Democratic Education in an Age of Difference

Richard Guarasci
Grant H. Cornwell
and Associates

Democratic Education in an Age of Difference

Redefining Citizenship in Higher Education

Jossey-Bass Publishers • San Francisco

Substantial discounts on bulk quantities of Jossey-Bass books are available to corporations, professional associations, and other organizations. For details and discount information, contact the special sales department at Jossey-Bass Inc., Publishers. (415) 433–1740; Fax (800) 605–2665.

For sales outside the United States, please contact your local Simon & Schuster International Office.
Jossey-Bass Web address: http://www.josseybass.com

 Manufactured in the United States of America on Lyons Falls Turin Book. This paper is acid-free and 100 percent totally chlorine-free.

Library of Congress Cataloging-in-Publication Data

Democratic education in an age of difference: redefining citizenship in higher education/[edited by] Richard Guarasci,
    Grant H. Cornwell.—1st ed.
        p. cm. — (The Jossey-Bass higher and adult education series)
    Includes bibliographical references (p. 171) and index.
    ISBN 0-7879-0850-9 (alk. paper)
    1. Citizenship—Study and teaching (Higher) —United States.
2. Multicultural education—United States. 3. Education, Higher—
Social aspects—United States. 4. Universities and colleges—United
States—sociological aspects. I. Guarasci, Richard. II. Cornwell,
Grant Hermans, date. III. Series.
LC1091.D398 1997
370.11′5—dc21
                                       96-37521

FIRST EDITION
HB Printing   10 9 8 7 6 5 4 3 2 1

The Jossey-Bass

Higher and Adult Education Series

Contents

To Tanner Cornwell,
whose presence in this project has been felt at every moment,
start to finish

For Carin, Bridget, and Patrick Guarasci,
and Peg, Kelsey, and Tosh Cornwell,
whose love sustains us and gives our lives meaning

Preface

Should undergraduate colleges prepare students for democratic citizenship? Should they seriously address issues of multicultural conflict on their campuses? Should increased ethnic, racial, and other forms of social diversity result in new campus and curricular programs? Will these new efforts foster the mission of preparing students for democratic citizenship? Or will they result in segregated and balkanized campuses that will further erode our belief in the ideal of "democratic education"? Will colleges and universities meet John Dewey's challenge to prepare students for active participation in shaping their education and their communities?

Democratic Education in an Age of Difference describes some of the programs underway that attempt to increase undergraduates' understanding of social differences while building a sense of campus community. As colleges and universities face the new challenges that increased social diversity has brought to campus life, these programs may be harbingers of a more effective approach to linking undergraduate academic development with citizenship education. They enhance our understanding of difference, democracy, and personal identity, while exploring their interdependence.

Faculty, administrators, educational policymakers, and others concerned about multiculturalism, citizenship education, and campus life will benefit from the detailed examples of campus efforts to address social diversity and community building provided here. The reader is offered concrete evidence of positive advances in the struggle to build an educational paradigm of social inclusion and citizenship education.

Critics of Multicultural Education

Contemporary critics of higher education charge that colleges too easily capitulate to the fashionable claims of any marginalized social group. They contend that higher education is prone to "political correctness" that forces a new liberal orthodoxy in the name of tolerance and openness. These critics argue that undergraduate education is in disrepair—that colleges and universities are unable or unwilling to prepare students adequately to think critically and act independently (Bloom, 1987).

If we accept these arguments, it would be reasonable to conclude that we suffer from "bad" colleges, that we are failing to prepare students to take their place in American society as the learned citizens and well-educated leaders necessary for an open and democratic society. The negative critique of colleges faults schools for overemphasizing the sociology of campus life instead of demanding excellence in education. To these critics the development of new approaches to learning, namely postmodernism, feminism, and radical social theory, have seriously eroded the foundations of American intellectual life: they have led students to believe that no universal truths exist, that all thought is relational, and that all behavior and morality is relative. The most intellectually substantive of these claims first appeared in Alan Bloom's *The Closing of the American Mind* (1987), and much of his critique has been mirrored in many conservative and critical texts (Atlas, 1990).

In contrast to these negative commentaries, this book provides illustrations of the essential work now under way in undergraduate education that points to a new paradigm for democratic learning. That new paradigm is not yet born, but we argue that some of the critical engagement of social and ethnic diversity on the campuses discussed here will lead the way to an approach to education appropriate for an increasingly diverse, politically democratic nation. We argue that education must be genuinely democratic throughout if it is to foster a viable understanding of and commitment to citizenship in a diverse democracy. We accent some of the conservative criticism, namely, that there is a need to refocus higher education on values, character, and citizenship, but we disagree strongly on the meaning of citizenship and on the means of realizing this educational goal.

We argue that a new citizenship must incorporate a fuller understanding of ethnic, racial, sexual orientation, and class differences, as well as a comprehensive history of these social differences and their interconnections in modern American society and on the global scene. Education for today's democracy in a more multicultural America must reacquaint students with the ideal of an inclusive, intercultural democracy. Toward this end students must learn how to demystify differences. We believe that experiential education is a powerful method for recognizing and honoring differences. And we believe that the arts of democracy—dialogue, engagement, and responsible participation—help students grow from intercultural experience and create democratic sensibilities.

Essential to this new democratic project is the development of curricular and co-curricular undergraduate experiences that open students not only to the nature and scope of difference but also to the interdependency of human experience. Only then will a new concept of democratic community be possible, one that understands difference and democracy to be complementary and that seeks inclusive commonality in which both legacy and uniqueness are secure and synergistic. Different from the communitarians' (Schlesinger, 1991; Etzioni, 1993) call for a superficial commonality that fears social differences as threats to a wholesome democracy, we argue that community and democratic citizenship are strengthened when undergraduates understand and experience social connections with those outside of their often parochial "autobiographies," and when they experience the way their lives are necessarily shaped by others. After all, democratic citizenship is about our obligations to one another; as more simply put in the old Quaker refrain, "We all belong to one another."

Overview of the Contents

As was mentioned previously, this book examines a number of interesting curricular and co-curricular initiatives in democratic education, a form of teaching and learning that accentuates critical reflection, active participation, the development of voice, and a deep commitment to social inclusion both in the classroom and the larger community.

In Chapter One, Richard Guarasci and Grant H. Cornwell outline the essential argument for a new "democratic sensibility" in undergraduate education. This sensibility prizes interculturalism and the interconnectedness of knowing and human experience. Unlike those writers who call for either a homogenized communitarianism or an essentialist and separatist notion of difference for its own sake, the authors discuss the complex nature of differences. They argue for a democratic community that builds on both differences and interdependency. Chapter One discusses the appropriateness of certain types of undergraduate education for this new educational project, namely interdisciplinary curricula, service learning, residential colleges, learning communities within the formal curriculum, and campus dialogues.

Chapter Two, written by Richard Guarasci, frames the argument for service learning as a potentially radical innovation for democratic education. When community involvement is joined to a rigorous curriculum and an ambitious reading and writing program, service learning holds the possibility of engendering a genuine understanding of difference and community. The focus of the chapter is on a comprehensive program of community-based learning at Hobart and William Smith Colleges (HWS) in upstate New York. By exploring the design and student experience of the HWS program, Guarasci illustrates the efficacy of public service learning for the new democratic project.

Chapter Three explores the particular promise of community learning for women's studies. Mary K. Trigg and Barbara J. Balliet chronicle their attempts to integrate feminist theory with community experience within the women's studies program at Rutgers University. They outline the ways in which students, submerged in feminist theory, test the promise and limits of that pedagogy when they encounter the complexity of women's lives in the communities around the university. Students begin to experience the myriad ways in which class and race intersect with gender and sexuality, often uncovering layers of particularity as well as unexpected commonality as they experience the real compression of choices available to women. These students also confront their own biases and parochialisms, ones they may have assumed they had long ago resolved for themselves.

Chapter Four, written by Grant H. Cornwell and Eve Stoddard, opens up the possibilities of an inclusive democratic paradigm that joins the academic and social lives of students into a holistic approach to learning and living. The authors discuss the history of the First-Year Program (FYP) at St. Lawrence University. In an unusual approach to liberal learning, the FYP requires discrete groups of students who share common housing to enroll in a year-long interdisciplinary common course dedicated to issues of community and difference. In very palpable ways, students' experiences in the residence are joined to a comprehensive menu of assigned texts, allowing students' lives to become a real laboratory for testing ideas and assumptions. In this sense, student autobiographies become a sort of additional text to be questioned and interpreted. The goal of the program is to create a democratic community.

In Chapter Five, Roberta S. Matthews and Daniel J. Lynch offer a related but different approach to the establishment of democratic education informed by deep social diversity; we learn about thematically clustered course packages for students at New York's LaGuardia Community College. LaGuardia is a two-year college populated by students drawn from an exceptionally diverse array of cultures. The students collectively speak more than forty-five native languages; most of them are first-generation college students and the sons and daughters of America's most recent immigrants. By grouping students in clusters, the program's engagement of social difference leads to a remarkable sense of social solidarity.

In Chapter Six, David Schoem offers a fascinating description of the University of Michigan's Program on Intergroup Relations, Conflict, and Community. The program is built around a new initiative called "intergroup dialogues," in which students engage "others" different from themselves. The expressed goal of the program is for students to "de-stereotype" their images of one another by joining personal experiences and untested and narrow assumptions with rich literature and autobiographical writing. The Michigan program offers yet another attempt to honor difference and forge human connection.

In the final chapter, Guarasci and Cornwell weave together the larger meaning of these projects. They glean from the individual cases a vision of what the landscape of teaching and learning would look like if colleges were transformed intentionally to meet their civic mission in a diverse democracy.

Acknowledgments

This book is a product of many minds. Insofar as it chronicles the work of many students, faculty, and staff on a number of campuses, it is important to acknowledge that many have assisted us in transforming the book from a concept to a completed text.

Rocco Capraro read Chapters One and Two and offered critical suggestions for their improvement. His wise advice has improved their merit significantly. His kind friendship added to the joy of their maturity. Eve Stoddard contributed a great deal to Chapter Seven. Her acumen, wit, and imagination make her all one could hope for in a collaborator.

Gale Erlandson provided much-needed editorial assistance. Her cogent comments and insightful suggestions improved the quality and content of the book. Rachel Livsey played a critical role in keeping our task on schedule. Jackie Hayes and Debbie Bishop contributed mightily to the final production of the text. Roberta Whitwood typed all of this manuscript through several drafts. Her patience and resiliency saw this project through to its completion. Her belief in the project strengthened the resolve of its authors to realize their initial vision for this book. We are forever indebted for her dedication. Our professional colleagues at our respective institutions indulged our need for time and space to complete the work.

Our families, to whom this book is dedicated, sustained us in our work and in our personal lives. Without them, this project would have been impossible.

February 1997   Richard Guarasci
Geneva, New York

Grant H. Cornwell
Canton, New York

The Authors

Richard Guarasci is provost and professor of political science at Wagner College. He was dean of Hobart College and professor of political science from 1992 through 1996. Previously he served on the faculty of St. Lawrence University from 1973 until 1992, where he was professor of political science and the founding director of the First-Year Program, and later the associate dean for university programs and academic affairs. He is the author of a number of publications, most recently concerned with higher education, citizenship education, and multiculturalism. He previously published pieces on American politics, labor policy, and social change. At present, Guarasci serves on the national board of directors of the Association of American Colleges and Universities as well as on boards of community organizations.

Grant H. Cornwell is associate dean and associate professor of philosophy at St. Lawrence University. He earned his B.A. degree with honors in biology and philosophy at St. Lawrence University, and his M.A. and Ph.D. degrees in philosophy at the University of Chicago. Cornwell's scholarly writing has focused on the epistemological and political dimensions of educational theory. He has published articles on radical pedagogy, multiculturalism, and postmodernism. He has received a number of awards for outstanding teaching, and has served on the board of directors of the American Association of Philosophy Teachers. He has also co-directed two national conferences sponsored by the Association of

American Colleges and Universities on cultural diversity and general education.

Contributors

Barbara J. Balliet received her Ph.D. degree in American history from New York University. Her edited collection *Women, Culture and Society* (1992) grew out of regular discussions among the faculty and graduate students teaching the introductory course in women's studies at Rutgers University. She is currently completing a book on gender and illustration in the nineteenth century.

Daniel J. Lynch is a professor of English at LaGuardia Community College of the City University of New York. He is a published novelist, short story writer, essayist, and poet. His mystery, *Ventry*, was published in 1990. He is a past president of the New York College English Association and a member of its conferences on ways of teaching writing, the nature of fiction, the use of computers in the classroom, and why some films are better than others.

Roberta S. Matthews, vice president for academic affairs at Marymount College in Tarrytown, New York, was the associate dean for academic affairs and professor of English at LaGuardia Community College of the City University of New York. She received her B.A. degree from Smith College, her M.A. degree from Columbia University, and her Ph.D. degree from the State University of New York at Stony Brook. Her publications on learning communities and collaborative learning include chapters in *Teaching and Learning in the Community College* (1993) and *Teaching on Solid Ground* (1995), and she has coauthored *Learning Communities: Creating Connections Among Students, Faculty and Disciplines* (1991), a chapter in *Handbook on the Undergraduate Curriculum* (1996), and *Bridging the Gap Between Cooperative and Collaborative Learning* (1995). Matthews is on the board of directors of the American Association for Higher Education, the Community College General Education Association, and American Social History Productions, Inc.

David Schoem is assistant dean for undergraduate education at the University of Michigan, lecturer in sociology, and co-director of the Program on Conflict Management Alternatives. He teaches courses in sociology such as "Intergroup Relations, Conflict, and Community," "Sociology of the American Jewish Community," and "Blacks and Jews: Dialogue on Ethnic Identity." Among his responsibilities as dean, he coordinates the college's undergraduate initiatives, the first-year seminar program, Michigan Learning Communities, and diversity initiatives in curriculum and instruction. He was also cofounder of Michigan's Program on Intergroup Relations, Conflict, and Community. Schoem is coeditor of *Multicultural Teaching in the University* (1993) and editor of *Inside Separate Worlds: Life Stories of Young Blacks, Jews, and Latinos* (1991). He received his B.A. degree from Michigan, his M.Ed. degree from Harvard, and his Ph.D. degree from the University of California at Berkeley.

Eve Stoddard serves as director of international and intercultural studies at St. Lawrence University. She received her A.B. degree from Mount Holyoke College and her Ph.D. degree in English from the University of California at Los Angeles. Trained as a specialist in Romantic literature and philosophy and in literary theory, she is now working on the topic of gender and race in the former British Empire. Over the past four years she has been working with faculty groups to develop a new paradigm of intercultural studies for the St. Lawrence curriculum.

Mary K. Trigg taught in the Rutgers women's studies program for five years, and inaugurated the course on women's community activism that accompanies the internship experience. She was most recently a visiting associate fellow with the Elizabeth Cady Stanton and Susan B. Anthony Papers Project in the history department at Rutgers. She earned her Ph.D. degree in American civilization from Brown University, and is now working on a project examining American feminism in the early twentieth century.

Democratic Education
in an Age of Difference

Chapter One

Democracy and Difference

Emerging Concepts of
Identity, Diversity, and Community

Richard Guarasci, Grant H. Cornwell

In many parts of the world, we are witnessing the renewal of democracy and the demand for greater democratic sensibility. With the opening of the former Soviet Union, the liberation of the vast region and peoples of Eastern Europe, the emergence of more procedurally democratic governments in a number of historically autocratic nations throughout Latin America, as well as any number of courageous and persistent movements for democratic order in such places as China, Korea, Kenya, and parts of the Middle East, this age will certainly be characterized as one of worldwide democratic expansion. And although many perceptive political analysts will carefully dissect the quality and depth of each of these situations in order more accurately to ascertain whether popular rule, civil and political rights, and social justice and public care really underscore the impact of these new realities, it is important to recognize that we live in a time when the desire for, if not the reality of, greater

This chapter first appeared as a farewell convocation address by Richard Guarasci at St. Lawrence University in August 1992. In a revised form it was delivered as a major address at the annual national meeting of the Association of American Colleges in January 1993. Another version appeared in print under joint authorship with Grant H. Cornwell in *Perspectives* (1993), the journal of the Association of General and Liberal Studies.

democratic order is an international impulse and one of the indelible identifying marks of this era.

But it is not the only indelible mark. We also live in a time when social distinctions and ethnic, racial, class, gender, and lifestyle differences have become even more critical to the way in which people identify themselves, experience the world around them, and make meaning of everyday life. We live in a time when our distinctions, our disconnections from one another, have become more important to some and more threatening to others than they have been at any other time certainly in the last half century. And rather than simply understanding these differences as something imposed on us, many people have embraced their differences as desirable, singular, and superior to those of people outside their immediate social orbits. As much as we live in an age celebrated for the renewal of democracy, we also live in an age that celebrates the social, ethnic, and racial differences that separate us from one another.

Here lies a fundamental and critical problem. In any of its conceptions, democracy is a system predicated on the concept of mutuality. It is a system of popular governance that assumes that a public exists from which popular, common sentiments will flow. Democracy is a way of associated living, in which reciprocity and connectedness are essential.

In traditional—both modern and classical—definitions of democracy, the prevailing subject is "we," but in a social world made up exclusively of sovereign, autonomous groups predicated on an exclusive disconnectedness, self-interest, and self-definition, "we" is replaced by an objective, distant, unknown "them." We owe much to recent feminist discourse for helping to acquaint many of our students with breaking down the "self-other" duality. Feminist scholarship has identified the ways in which traditional education fails to address adequately the importance of difference. This research warns us of how each of us may view differences and how we can characterize those different from us as "the others," the inferior and the threatening.

But in an age when democracy is becoming renewed and difference for its own sake is becoming the outcome of democratic uprisings, it is likely that the mutuality and reciprocity necessary for democratic order will minimally be undone by this other prevailing need for difference. In short, our traditional visions of democracy are unable to point the way to peace and prosperity in a world that also wishes to be founded on the primacy of difference.

When only difference matters—no matter how well intended—those who are different, those who can be categorized as "them," the "other," can be more easily ignored, oppressed, and abused. We see this being played out nationally and internationally, but we also are witness to it in a spate of contemporary campus conflicts. The personal wounds run deep in these exchanges, and the damage to community life is profound.

This is the human face of the new American dilemma of reconciling the ideal of democratic community in an age now institutionalizing difference as an end itself. In the United States, we are celebrating a democratic community of differences, but we are also witnessing an experience of resegregation.

What is needed is a wholly different ideal of the democratic community in which both difference *and* connection can be held together yet understood to be at times necessarily separate, paradoxical, and in contradiction to one another. We need new definitions of democracy, community, and difference. Our old definitions of these concepts are unable to offer us a vision of a new kind of community that prizes our multiplicity. Both individually and in groups we hold many simultaneous identities as men and women, as members of ethnic and racial groups, as professional and service workers. We need nonlinear concepts that recognize our multilayered society, a society in which any individual may hold many subidentities at once and in which power, prestige, and social standing are multiplicious and nonhierarchical. In short, we need a concept of a multicentric democracy in which the concept and experience of self and others are as connected as they are distinct and singular.

Difference

But before we embark on reconceptualizing the ideal of democratic community it is imperative that we study the meaning and nature of difference in our present historical and national context. Certainly in this society, as in most, differences are multiple. They rarely exist so singularly as to produce such dualities as self and other, black and white, I and thou. Most differences are highly influenced by the context in which they appear. Circumstances—place and time—often determine what is different about anyone.

For instance, an African American, upper-middle-class male in the midst of a gathering in a black community would likely be seen as different because of class and gender, not because of race. The same man in a gathering of white professionals will likely identify himself as a person of color first, a man second, and less likely as a member of the upper–middle class.

A white working-class woman in a white working-class community will be distinctive by gender rather than by class or race. If we factor in lifestyle, sexual preference, occupation, and other meaningful social, economic, ethnic, and racial categories, then our identities become even more obviously multiple. This is not to say that all differences are equal in our society, nor is it to deny the long-continuing and painful oppression imposed on any one identity; rather it is to appreciate what educator Catherine Stimpson has put so aptly: "That our society is so complex and differentiated that each of us belongs, not simply to a majority or a minority, but to several majority and minority groups at once" (Stimpson, 1992b, p. 77).

Identity politics ultimately becomes reduced to interest group cultural politics; groups not only take identity in their race, gender, sexual orientation, or ethnicity but also take too much status from their victimization as a central element of their personal identity. Identity politics can lead to a reactionary habituation to the social status quo, in which meaning is derived from oppression. It can become all of experience rather than part of it; when this happens, inwardness and cultural isolation are seen as not only preferred but necessary.

When we substitute moral reasoning for identity politics, the ultimate objective is justice. Moral reasoning allows us to develop a discourse and a politics that bridge the formerly remote distances of separate cultural oppressions by recognizing the multiple types of victimization. Moral reasoning opens room for any of us to carry around the many primary and secondary social identities important to us and to engage these various identities within our groups as well as across them. In such a political environment conflict could be acknowledged, understood, and engaged without reproducing the entire construct of racial oppression and political subordination. In contrast, by building a singular politics of difference and by failing to recognize that differences are multiple, we more likely maintain political marginalization and sustain individual repression. What results is less a politics of liberation and more an "aria" of personal dislocation.

The Scope of Difference

To understand more fully how one type of difference can become predominant, if not paralyzing, one needs to explore in depth the way race has always maintained an enduring influence on social experience and identity in the United States.

Although many literary and social critics have captured this American tragedy, new images of racial oppression never cease to compel one's imagination. Perhaps this is because racial injustice is in direct opposition to the American ideology of freedom of choice and the pursuit of happiness.

In *Two Nations: Black and White, Separate, Hostile, Unequal,* Andrew Hacker (1992) offers us a graphic statistical array of the costs of racism. He compiles tables demonstrating dramatic income differentials by race, regardless of educational background, occupation, and geography. He portrays the black unemployment rate as maintaining its historic figure of two and a half times the white rate of unemployment. He cites how African Americans are dramatically underrepresented as lawyers, physicians, and architects, as well as waiters, bartenders, and dental hygienists (apparently, these latter positions are too public for some employers)—all of this in an era of affirmative action.

Even more alarming, almost forty years after the landmark *Brown* vs. *the Board of Education* Supreme Court decision, the overwhelming majority of African American children attend virtually segregated schools. For example, in Illinois, New York, Michigan, California, New Jersey, and Maryland the percentage of black children attending virtually segregated schools ranges from 72 percent in Maryland up to 83 percent in Illinois. In New York, the most liberal state in many social policies, 81 percent of all African American children attend virtually segregated schools. Not surprisingly, 86 percent of all white suburban children attend virtually segregated schools. In 1990, New York City schools came close to resembling Mississippi schools in 1960. And upon entering college, the students from these various schools meet each other as virtual strangers from the same country. The most compelling statistic of all shows that the majority of African American males between the ages of sixteen and twenty-four are under the supervision of some part of the American criminal justice system (Hacker, 1992).

Racism reduces difference to a single dimension of identity, and as such it may leave us a nation of strangers, where we are all disconnected, some are victimized, and where color or ethnicity becomes an excuse to oppress. As the philosopher Cornel West has written recently, "to engage in a serious discussion of race in America we must begin *not* with the problems of black people but with the flaws of American society—flaws rooted in historic inequalities and longstanding stereotypes. . . . As long as black people are viewed as 'them' . . . as only different . . . then change will avoid us" (West, 1994b, p. 6).

If we were to explore gender, the other paramount difference in U.S. society, we would view an equally dramatic portrait. Although some economic differentials are relenting, income, employment, mobility, and poverty statistics demonstrate the remarkable resiliency of systematic and enduring gender inequality (Gilligan, 1982; Hochschild, 1989). As with the study of cultural differences, rich literary and social analyses written during the last decade have demonstrated the very real differences between men and women in social experience and in psychological, social, ethical, and cognitive development.

Clearly, difference is a central fact in our lives. Our experiences as persons of a particular race and gender are critical and, in some sense, defining. But they are not singular, nor are they the whole of experience. And although the studies of gender differences may demonstrate that we are as much strangers in our most intimate private lives as we are unequal in our public ones, these differences do not foreclose our connectedness across racial and gender lines.

The acknowledgment and celebration of difference is necessary but insufficient in the project of human liberation. We must *begin* with difference so that the unique experiences of self, gender, and race will break the long silences resulting from the conjunction of difference and oppression. But if we remain in these early stages of resistance, and elevate difference to mean superiority in the pursuit of self-esteem and (ultimately) power, we risk reproducing the very systems of inequality responsible for oppression and domination.

As much as we need to reconceptualize our understanding of community and of democracy so that they can embrace and sustain uniqueness and self, so we must also reconceptualize our understanding of difference. A new understanding of difference must capture its complexity by including multiplicity, connectedness, and reciprocity. Without a broader definition, our era will be recalled as one of democratic renewal founded on the celebration of difference that gives sanction to the already powerful and privileged. This will lead us to accept old ideologies that habituate us to the inevitability of difference as the most distinctive feature of social life.

Community and Multiplicity

Feminist poet Audre Lorde has written, "Difference must not merely be tolerated but seen as a fund of necessary polarities, . . .

only then does the necessity of interdependence become unthreatening" (Lorde, 1984, pp. 115–116). She helps us understand the need to integrate both difference and connection: we cannot get to a healthy democratic community without realizing how the recognition and reality of difference must be part of that community's foundation. Different from classical and modern definitions of democracy, we must build a multicentric democratic vision. Neither Rousseau's democratic order as an overarching common identity nor Locke's minimalist conception of a collection of separate self-interests aggregated into a limited state will suffice as a proper vision for the type of democracy necessary today. As Charles Taylor (1992) has persuasively argued, the limitations of "procedural liberalism" in the teeth of the growing multicultural nature of most societies make it an unlikely method of governance for the future world. According to Taylor, more of society's members "live the life of Diaspora, whose center is elsewhere[;] . . . the challenge is to deal with their sense of marginalization without compromising our basic political principles" (p. 63).

We need a democratic order that can contain the contradiction of difference and connection, self and community, one and many. It must be democracy in which commonality is understood as negotiated and constructed, not inherited or natural. This is a community in which paradox, contradiction, and ambiguity can be appreciated rather than feared. Because creating the new democratic order requires fundamental change in individual and social behaviors, we must look to our educational systems as the logical place to effect the reforms we need.

Democratic Education in an Age of Difference

What type of education would promote the objectives of democracy? Multicentric education requires certain critical skills and some habits of mind long associated with a liberal arts education. To become active participants in public life and democratic decision making, students must develop the "arts" of democracy. These include an appreciation for open inquiry and the development of communication skills. Students must learn how to find their own voices and how to construct arguments. They need to distinguish arguments from opinions by relying on evidence. Ultimately students need to make judgments based on wisdom and knowledge rather than on prejudice and parochialism. These are many of the traditional skills associated with liberal learning. In short, multicentric education is founded on an appreciation for complexity as a means to understand multiplicity. Multicentric education helps us to appreciate ambiguity, contradiction, and nuance, and prepares us to accept the coexistence of difference and sameness.

A rich liberal arts education will contribute to each of the aforementioned qualities. The study of the sciences, the humanities, the arts, and the social sciences requires the use of all of these attributes to fully master these subjects. But these qualities, while necessary, are not sufficient in and of themselves for a world of multicentrism. What is required above and beyond this training is a wholesale immersion in those studies that accentuate the interconnectedness of human experience. Multicentric education requires a curriculum that *also* focuses on the interplay of community and difference, or what radical educator Henry Giroux calls "border studies, the points of intersection, where different histories, languages, experiences and voices intermingle amidst diverse relations of power and privilege" (Giroux, 1992, p. 209).

Interdisciplinary Studies and General Education

The world of interdisciplinary studies is where connection, integration, and synthesis are prized. Interdisciplinary studies call for a curricular design and a college experience in which interculturalism is the very means of forging connectedness, mutuality, and common destiny. Students are introduced to a new view of commonality—commonality founded on the equality of different voices and stories, commonality that acknowledges the past, addresses the new, and envisions the possible. With intercultural understanding, different pasts will allow us to envision a common future. This becomes the focus of much of the interdisciplinary general education curriculum, which works in ways that expand the power of the disciplines without denying them their own specificity.

Historically, the movement toward democratic education at the collegiate level was interwoven with that of general education (Miller, 1988). As a reaction to the growing phenomena of overspecialization and departmentalization, the general education movement of the thirties sought to reaffirm the need for an integrated undergraduate education. This movement developed along two lines.

One approach, championed by Robert Hutchins (1936), called for a renewed commitment to a more classical education founded on what Hutchins referred to as the great conversation. The curriculum was its focus and the so-called great books its substance. The goal was to rid higher education of its fetish with progress and empiricism, which according to Hutchins resulted in anti-intellectualism and, to some degree, in faddish superficiality. He wanted to cultivate the classical intellectual virtues such as philosophical wisdom, art, and induction. At the University of Chicago, he created a separate college based on general education. Later at St. John's College, the great books movement found an institution solely dedicated to this approach.

Alexander Meiklejohn took the concept of general education in quite another direction from that of Hutchins (Meiklejohn, 1932). Believing as Hutchins did that undergraduates needed an integrated education, Meiklejohn sought to find an educational model that prized intelligence less for its own sake but rather as a necessity for the social development of the nation. He wanted an educational experience that allowed intelligence to be applied to contemporary problems. To Meiklejohn, "intelligence . . . is readiness for any human situation; it is the power, wherever one goes, of being able to see, in any set of circumstances, the best response which a human being can make of those circumstances" (1932, p. 5). He wanted an integrated education of social as well as intellectual development that would cultivate a habit of social action and democratic community making. Central to his thought was the need for special emphasis on the development, not the imposition, of character. He believed that higher education must be sensitive more to the context and less to the content of the curriculum (Miller, 1988, p. 44).

Hutchins and Meiklejohn raised fundamental questions, however, about the social nature of learning in the post World War II expansion of higher education. Their themes were submerged beneath the need for mass access to college and the rise of the disciplines. A tremendous amount of curricular and co-curricular reform has occurred in the last decade, but what we find most interesting are the number of attempts to create democratic initiatives within traditional institutions.

In addition to the reemergence of interdisciplinary general education, two other efforts aimed at addressing colleges as social communities are quite instructive and hold genuine possibilities for helping us develop a pedagogy appropriate for a multicentric democratic society.

Community-Based Learning

One advance is the resurgence of community service on many college campuses. It is imperative that students begin to learn about the immediate world in which they live, namely the campus community and its surroundings. Through community service many students encounter persons and contexts quite distinct from their own experience, which helps them understand more fully the "self-other" dichotomy. Students see how they are both different from and yet similar to others outside their immediate biographies; they begin to comprehend how self-respect and regard for others are intimately linked both in their development and in the needs of the communities in which they live.

Toward these ends, participation in community service becomes a potentially transformative educational experience for undergraduates. As experiential learning that intentionally aims to assist others in meeting needs, service to others connects our students to immediate experiences of everyday life faced by those different from them (at least insofar as the community members are not college students), and teaches them to view the world from sometimes remarkably different perspectives. Service to others asks our students to take account of the world outside themselves. It asks them to contemplate the range of economic, political, and historical forces that shape the choices available to the local communities and particular individuals involved in the students' community work.

Most important, service to others develops within our students an ethic of care. Such work is fundamentally a commitment to recognize and honor the voices as well as the needs of others. And as our mission statements clearly state, the moral and ethical development of undergraduates constitutes one of the central ends of a liberal arts education. In the context of service learning, moral growth occurs as an outgrowth of the dialogue between students and community residents, as each share their values and histories together. In this context the development of undergraduate character is shaped from encounter and experience with the world as well as with the ideas that form the intellectual foundation of the university curriculum, as opposed to the more traditional notion of moral development as the didactic imposition of beliefs, values, and required behavior.

Residential Learning Communities

A second advance are the many attempts to reunify student life with the formal curriculum. Exclusive reliance on the formal curriculum to provide the spine for a community of learners is at best problematic. In a world where more than three-quarters of the students representative of distinct races and ethnic groups are educated in virtually segregated high schools, the formal curriculum will likely not replace the overarching need for common living experiences as a means of allowing students to engage fully with voices and histories distinct from their own. If ever undergraduate education needed a pedagogical model that recombined learning and life inside and outside the classroom, it is at this juncture in college history. Reconnecting intellectual life with the social and communal development of students is now more than a luxury: it is an imperative for any undergraduate institution that takes seriously its larger obligations to this society and to the full development of its students.

On a growing number of campuses, faculties and administrative leaders are proposing and implementing various strategies for connecting student life and the formal curriculum. One method calls for the development of residential colleges within the campus community, where students who live together share one or more common courses. Here the experience of common intellectual engagement can become a compelling opportunity for students to encounter one another as persons as well as students. All of the issues surrounding difference and community—embedded in the racial, gender, ethnic, sexual orientation, and other cultural and social idiosyncrasies of students—form a parallel curriculum that can be informed by a common discourse emanating from the students' shared formal curriculum. In many ways, residential colleges and living-learning models allow students to begin to explore their own lives and their common situation as texts unto themselves.

The Role of Faculty

Interdisciplinary education, community service, and residential colleges all call upon the pedagogy of connection and community founded on the necessity of difference. They are means for realizing an undergraduate experience appropriate for a multicentric democracy.

In multicentric education, faculty are critical role models. We cannot ask students to achieve what we ourselves are incapable of achieving, namely, to recognize, value, and negotiate differences. If the faculty choose to isolate themselves, to allow themselves to be victims of what Catherine Stimpson (1992a) calls disciplinary narcissism, to allow themselves to become immersed in fights over resources, then they are reneging on their obligation to teach students that learning liberates us from isolation and frees us to engage with the world and not just live in it. If faculty fail to demonstrate how learning is about conversation and about the ability to enlarge that discourse continually, they will fail our students; they will be teaching them that learning is only about institutional politics and not about the expansion of human personality.

Without this type of multicentric curriculum and absent a collegial faculty up to the task of teaching it, democratic education will fail to prepare our students either for the world of difference or to the difference multicentric education can make for the building of a viable democratic community.

Democratic Education and the Academic Workplace

As Audre Lorde (1984) has said about difference and community, the imperative of recognizing the multiplicity of differences within society inevitably requires that we simultaneously acknowledge them within ourselves. When we encounter the "other" within our own personality, we are then prepared to engage the other in those around us. Masculine and feminine, racial and ethnic, differing orientations—all become less subordinating dualities and more existential differences to be understood and engaged.

So too within institutions. Difference and community can be experienced less as threats or panaceas for the contours of the curriculum or the allocation of resources. The contemporary academy is no more prepared for the enclosing world of interculturalism than the society that surrounds it. As a refraction of that society, colleges and universities retain a structure of authority and an organization of academic work quite compatible with the minimalist democratic tradition of Locke. Framed on a governance reminiscent of the liberal state but infused with corporatist and bureaucratic history, modern colleges are less the romanticized learning communities of the distant past and more like seemingly ungovernable cities of the modern day. As such they are more likely to *accommodate* difference—departmental, divisional, school, as well as ethnic and social—than to *engage* it as a means to construct something closer to a community of both learning and citizenship.

Although university and college bashing has become popular reading of late (and some of these criticisms are warranted), we must also acknowledge that colleges by and large reflect the social values, and the social and moral confusion, that surround them. Colleges are not privileged islands apart from society. As liberal society has opted for a political culture in which autonomy and prosperity are its essential values, freedom in higher education may have its metaphor in a sometimes rigid tenure system (placing many professors beyond serious performance review after only seven years in the profession). Specialized knowledge and the explosion of scientific research are marbled in departmental and divisional separations that many times result in a disconnected and somewhat incoherent undergraduate experience as well as balkanized and byzantine academic politics. Administration is often limited to a role similar to that of the minimalist liberal state, that is, being nothing more than a neutral process authorized to sort out competing claims for limited resources. In fact, administrators who develop vision and mission statements are often considered suspect (or are ignored) by fellow administrators and by faculty. Administration that only "administers" erroneously equates management with leadership.

Clearly the development of a new educational vision and a genuine experience with democracy, community, and difference must begin with changes in the administration of colleges and universities. William Tierney (1989) has written persuasively about the need for transformative leadership in higher education; many examples of such leadership exist in universities and colleges. Transformative administrators lead institutions to develop clear missions, stated goals and objectives, and positive assessment processes. Most important, these administrators recognize how to integrate the diverse work and learning cultures within their institutions into a focused, dedicated, and respectful institutional heritage.

As Lorde (1984) suggests for each of us, "difference and interdependence" must be recognized as essential elements of our personalities if we are to be prepared for the worlds around us. Nothing short of a different type of collegial citizenship will be required for the coming era of higher education if we are to go beyond the limits of accommodation and realize a period of genuine transformation. Change of such magnitude will involve redefinitions of authority and responsibility on campus for faculty, administration, and students, and such educational reform will occur only through educational experiences aimed at addressing democracy on and off campus. Such experiences and programs are now underway. The goal of this book's authors is to foster the conversation about them and further underscore the importance of understanding their significance.

Chapter Two

Community-Based Learning and Intercultural Citizenship

Richard Guarasci

Although we live in a world that is obsessed with difference as both sanctuary and threat, reliance on the politics of difference and separation is a doomed strategy. The politics of difference fails to produce a democratic community and it fails as an enduring means to personal liberation as well. If democratic education holds any genuine meaning for our present political circumstance, it must be as a powerful vessel in our passage to a reconstructed multicentric democratic order. To this end democratic education must assist us in the broader project of redefining the meanings of democracy, community, and difference, such that each retains its essential elements.

Without some basic commitment to the larger relationship of all of us to one another, citizenship is reduced to the narrow confines of voting, limited rights, taxes, or what Ben Barber aptly labels "thin democracy" (1993, p. 169). And in this era of interculturalism, democracy without some basic allegiance to recognizing social difference is likely to reduce quickly to one of two possibilities. Either it will become an oppressive centralized force imposing an unnecessary ideological or ethnic rigidity on the whole, usually in the service of the parochial interests of the powerful; or it will be ignored as a toothless process able only to receive an endless array of demands from competing groups, each claiming inherent rights without any understanding of reciprocal obligations. In failing to incorporate community *and* difference both versions of democracy are untenable and unlikely to be sustained.

Democracy needs to be framed by high degrees of civic and political participation, through which shared experience will more likely reduce the "threat" from difference and allow for the beginnings of a positive sense of reciprocity. In the absence of any fundamental common experience, we can be sure there will be no felt common purpose. Strangers become feared "others" and then either threatening competitors or, worse, social pariahs.

This new democracy will only become viable with a new understanding of citizenship, one that goes beyond the current American experience of the citizen as simply voter and taxpayer. We are implying a contemporary variant of the somewhat romanticized image of the citizen portrayed in classical and political theory. What we are after is a new democratic sensibility in which citizens' participation extends well beyond the narrowly governmental activities of elections, campaigns, lobbying, and protest. In this fuller sense of citizenship one feels both rights *within* and responsibilities *to* the larger community, while also sensing some equally powerful and obligatory necessity for protecting the health and welfare of those groups that constitute difference. Ultimately citizenship reaffirms the notion that we all "belong" to one another.

This approach calls for a democratic order, one akin to Dewey's belief in democracy as a "mode of associated living, of conjoint communicated experience" ([1916] 1966, p. 87). We need to imagine this type of democracy as expansive, inclusive, and participatory. Our understanding of citizenship is informed by this larger sense of engagement and commitment, so that the dialogue and experience Dewey emphasizes become central and foundational. Here citizenship is not limited to the legalistic narrowness of rights and obligations but rather extends to a fuller notion of active involvement and equal standing within a political and social community.

And there is more to Dewey's short but pregnant definition. Community is not merely a concept of assumed commonalities, some assumption of homogenized values as inherited or assumed to be natural and true. Dewey's emphasis on "associated living" and "conjoint communicated experiences" speaks to a dynamic interplay of social and communal moments in and around neighborhoods, schools, churches, and all the organizations in which public life is negotiated and defined. People are crossing the borders of class, ethnicity, religion, gender, sexual orientation, and all the other aspects that shape personality, identity, and experience. Through conflict and engagement, the democratic public order is negotiated within the plurality of languages and varieties of experience represented within the larger community. Predicated on an assumption of equality and active citizen participation, the three components of dialogue, communication, and social experience form the basis for democratic living.

To approach so expansive an ideal requires at the very least an inspired democratic imagination. Moreover, this ideal necessitates a democratic sensibility—an act of faith in the inherent possibility of positive social action and a general disposition of optimism. This sensibility allows human actions to shape and reshape the life of the community while also allowing individuals to define themselves through personal action and interaction.

But it must become more than a romantic ideal. It must surpass the uncritical optimism of Dewey's conception of democratic community and allow for what Cornel West (1993a) identifies as the tragic and self-destructive in our character. West has warned us about building too hopeful a democratic faith, one separated from reality by what he describes as "a profound sense of evil" (p. 45). After all, human choice and moral action are what will chart the actual course of democratic societies, and a multicentric society will require the development of personal sensibilities formed in cooperative, multicultural, and layered social experiences.

Clearly this multicentric society is one founded on a new ethic. It is one in which healthy competition is balanced by cooperation and caring. As Nell Noddings (1984) convincingly argues, society needs to be based on a moral sensibility that ultimately rests on an experience of connectedness. Without inclusivity, we will be without any meaningful and appropriate new sense of justice. Without a new meaning of justice, there will be no new understanding of citizenship. But just as we reincarnate older definitions of republican civic virtue, Audre Lorde's words remind us that just any connections won't do: "Too often, we pour the energy needed for recognizing and exploring difference into pretending those differences are insurmountable barriers, or that they do not exist at all. This results in a voluntary isolation, or false and treacherous connections. Either way, we do not develop tools for using human difference as a springboard for creative change within our lives. We speak not of human difference, but of human deviance (1984, pp. 115–116)."

Homogenized commonality is the enemy of respect for difference, identity, and privacy. It allows no quarter for difference or multiplicity because its only social glue is sameness. At the same time, we need a new ethic of caring rooted in an understanding of justice not founded on the old dualities of competing differences. This new ethic must be more open ended, more inclusive, more experiential, so that we may more fully reconcile the social realities of an intercultural and multicentric society. A more fully participatory citizenship, one that embraces this understanding and reconciliation, will require more everyday skills in negotiating contradiction, ambiguity, and nuance.

As we bring forward a new paradigm of democratic education appropriate for this emerging interculturalism, experiential learning will by necessity play a central, critical role in acquainting both teachers and learners about the particulars of difference in any specific context, and in honing the pedagogy of multicentric democracy. If we connect the classroom to the world around it by using experiences as "texts," we will demystify differences by finding their common human seams while simultaneously recognizing their authentic uniqueness. As Lorde (1984, pp. 115–116) puts it, we will then "develop the tools" to break the seeming "insurmountable barriers" of difference and end the destructive force of invisibility brought on by parochialism and false homogenization. By direct encounter and experience, students and teachers increase their comfort with the "other," with the "different," as they begin to see their connection to difference as well as its presence within themselves. This is Lorde's "springboard for creative change within our [own] lives."

Community, Education, and Service

One very promising means for reconnection lies in the present renaissance of service learning. Although the popular media and many of the contemporary images of the adolescent and the young adult project a portrait of an empty generation prone to narcissism, anger, and violence, a good deal of hard data indicate that a significant core of that same generation is invested in altruistic and civic activities in the service of troubled communities and vulnerable individuals (Campus Compact, 1995).

Many college students participate in coordinated programs of community service. According to Campus Compact, a coalition of 520 college and university presidents committed to service learning, many millions of hours of service are dedicated to such work by college students. Based on a survey of member institutions, Campus Compact found that more than 321,000 students at its 520 member schools were involved in weekly service in the 1994–95 academic year. The organization estimates that over nineteen million hours of public service were performed by college students in the 1994–95 academic year (Campus Compact, 1995). In addition to the vast range of volunteer activities in and around college campuses, 87 percent of the Campus Compact colleges offered service learning courses, with an average of fifteen classes at each school.

The Campus Outreach Opportunity League (COOL), founded in 1983, is a student service organization that maintains alliances with students and faculty at more than 650 colleges and universities. The Partnership for Service Learning offers academic credit programs recognized by 150 colleges. Other key student service organizations include SCALE, the national student literacy campaign, and the National Campaign Against Hunger and Homelessness. Many other organizations flourish at the local and campus level, such as the popular City Year in Boston. Clearly there exists within this generation of students the will for social connection and civic community.

The prime motivation for many of these student volunteers rests in a moral commitment to help those expressing need for assistance. They see the immediate world around them populated by too many people caught in the cruel inequalities and misfortunes of modern societies. They are compelled to personal action.

Lisa Kelly, a recent graduate of Notre Dame, was moved to action when her work-study job in a college cafeteria had her filling large bins with leftover food for garbage removal. After stopping into a local office for community concerns one evening after work, she found others who could help her appropriate this quite edible food for those truly in need, the local homeless. She helped found Foodshare, which served over twenty thousand meals in its first year (Commission on National and Community Service, 1993). As Van Troung Le, a recent alumnus of Harvard, states, "Substantial community work is the best ethical training you can get" (Commission on National and Community Service, 1993, p. 52). Van Troung Le's work with the homeless is well chronicled by the commission.

Beyond the imperative of moral witness, service holds the promise of teaching students about civic participation and about what I have called democratic sensibility. As students develop a habit of service that they will take with them when they graduate, they are building a critical experience in expanded citizenship. They are developing a greater commitment to social interdependence, reciprocity, and a common destiny with all those "others" who inhabit their immediate social and professional orbits. As a Rutgers student aptly expressed it, "We pretty much feel that you just can't keep taking from society. I really feel that students are starting to realize that in order to solve the economic problems, you really have to have social responsibility" (Commission on National and Community Service, 1993, p. 8).

But beyond these essential and laudable efforts of community service, the present renewal in civic participation holds the possibility of bringing students into contact with communities, individuals, and circumstances far from the confines of the students' parochial biographies. As mentioned in Chapter One, Hacker's data on the socioeconomic composition of secondary education indicates that new college students are virtually strangers to one another (1992). Their life experience is mostly limited along class, racial, and ethnic lines. Their personal experience with social difference is at best unrefined and subject to the most formulaic of activities. The ideal of community, if ever realized, is often limited to the cultural histories of their immediate circumstance. Public service introduces students to persons, stories, languages, and legacies well beyond the scope of their experience. It engages them outside of their world of campus life and late adolescence. Within the intimacies of these moments they engage persons with problems that at first seem disarmingly remote but that ultimately present them with compelling connections. By virtue of age, gender, race, ethnicity, or just a sense of shared vulnerability, service experience may engender the embryo of difference, multiplicity, and common bond. Our understanding of commonality is there for the learning if contextualized and interpreted, especially when shared with others similarly involved and part of a larger, structured learning opportunity.

Public service holds the power of real experiences, which are generally internalized and understood as stories and metaphors for larger social relations. Through service learning, connections are found and meanings made amid the profound differences and similarities among the lives of citizens in turbulence and the lives of volunteers, many of which reflect disequilibrium and deep vulnerabilities themselves. By joining ethnographies of community residents with the autobiographical portraits of the students, a powerful pedagogy of service begins to uncover the recesses of private life, exposing authentic cultural identities amid a not insignificant well of commonalities and overlapping experiences and histories. Multiplicity and commonality are recovered in the collection of private biographies. From these types of pedagogical innovations, service learning courses allow students and residents to be stitched together into a fabric of mutuality and common purpose.

At its best, democratic education joins ideas and experience in a dialogical interplay that produces critical interpretation and encourages imagination. It is founded on social exchange within groups that ultimately create communities of learning in which ideas and experiences are scrutinized, reinterpreted, and evaluated. The process of democratic education unites the process of learning with the substantive content of rigorous scholarship. At its best it produces a metaphor for democratic community itself, in which voice, participation, and ultimately action are joined into a civics of learning. As the participants reflect greater differences among themselves by virtue of their idiosyncratic autobiographies, democratic education fosters thinking, listening, and speaking skills evocative of the traditions of liberal education. Service learning, when framed by an intentional program of reflection and interpretation, is one method for realizing the promise of democratic education. It must be accompanied by a vision of service compatible with liberal education, and it must be drawn out by nothing short of a pedagogy of community-based learning.

Community-Based Learning: A Pedagogy for Citizenship

Service learning becomes community-based learning under specific arrangements. It is more than voluntary service performed by students isolated from any intimate relationship with course content and class discussion. It is certainly more than community involvement by students whose participation is merely accidental to the curricular component. By definition, service learning requires an intentional curricular connection. When student community work is joined to a defined course content, integrated into the classroom dialogue, and linked to a set of community partners involved in the course discussion, then service learning becomes authentic community-based learning. When service learning approaches this standard it becomes citizenship education.

The goals of this type of learning are multiple. In focusing on the construction of participatory citizenship, service learning is about the reconciliation of those false differences that erode the possibility of inclusive communitarianism. Learning begins with the rediscovery of social empathy. All ethical education must first locate this basic instinct for human decency. The mere proximity and interaction of seemingly disparate individuals around the immediate problems of social need are likely to create the conditions for meaningful human connection. Demystification of the "other" becomes a possibility, although by no means a probability.

But service learning that approaches citizenship education must reach well beyond the necessary preconditions of increased empathy among its student and community participants. It must approach issues of social boundaries, personal identity, justice, political efficacy, and community building. To forge this type of learning, not only must the experience within the community be brought into a critical reflection by the individual student, but it also must be contextualized within the larger issues often hidden from the narrow volunteer experience of the student. This requires a curricular context provided by poignant readings and reflective assignments, and critical discussion of the various social and individual values at the center of the service experience. Without the benefit of the larger context afforded by powerful readings, clear assignments, and class discussions, the individual volunteer experience becomes prisoner to the limits of the private world of the solitary student. Its transformative impact is seriously reduced.

Curricular experiences that address the goals of ethical development, critical reflection, and community participation necessarily require a comprehensive pedagogy. Because of its field component, service learning is a form of experiential learning. This particular feature suggests much of the pedagogical approach necessary for a fully comprehensive service learning program. Experiential learning requires attention to active learning strategies capable of deepening the analysis and interpretation of the student's field experience.

Other pedagogical elements prove to be quite complementary to community-based learning. Collaborative work blends well with this type of learning. Students working in teams, particularly when volunteering at the same field site, allow for enhanced critical assessment of the context and meaning of students' experiences. They find ways to forge a significant dialogue about persons and situations they encounter in the community. Combined with an integrated approach to texts and classroom discussions, the field work is placed within a much broader intellectual and moral context.

In addition, intensive writing and autobiographical assignments integrate the full meaning of community-based learning. Writing is a form of knowing and thinking. Communication, experience, and reflection are the means to intellectual and ethical growth. Writing, reading, and—as important—action are the means to this growth. In community-based learning all three forms of knowing bring service learning classes together so that students can share and compare their thoughts and feelings. To these ends course assignments provide moments for communication and reflection in which students can personally engage the course content—both the reading and the service—and begin to create a community of learning *within* the course. Writing assignments in and outside the classroom help students to collaborate in ways that enable them to expand their personal understanding of their common experience and then to fashion their community involvement as a collective and cooperative pedagogy of community-based learning. Different types of assignments—analytic, dialogical journals, field notes, ethnographies, and autobiographical reflections—all form a larger mosaic of values, ideas, theory, and knowledge such that cognitive and ethical growth result from a social pedagogy of learning.

The final piece to this method may be unique to community-based learning. It involves the integration of community members into the course itself, particularly as they come to understand the means and ends of the larger educational project. As community members become fully engaged in the larger goals of the course and help students and instructors wed those goals to the needs and hopes of the community, they become in essence teachers themselves. They help us expand the size of the "faculty" as they offer our students additional and critical voices speaking about the nature of the course subject matter and the existential realities present in the immediate community. The menu of choices available to the community becomes as real in the classroom as it is on the street, where the economic, political, social, and historical domains join, and where possibilities and real contradictions meet. Here the juncture of personal autobiography and social history are vivid, and students can witness it firsthand.

A pedagogy of community-based learning brings all of this to the table: experiential, active, and collaborative learning; intensive writing and reading; autobiographical work; ethical and value-centered education; peer learning; and the expansion of the "faculty" by the integration of the community into the course. These methods set the stage for deep and rich learning; students can be teachers and learners as well as agents for social justice and participatory citizenship. This type of learning allows for a full tapestry of intellectual inquiry, cultural encounter, and personal reflection.

Contours and Issues

Not all service learning aims explicitly to engage issues of social difference and democratic community. Some service learning—incredibly important to value-based and ethical education—lies outside the particular focus of race, gender, class, and other social identities. Most of service learning, however, does address the issues of social responsibility surrounding a particular community and a particular discipline. Here we are concerned with the type of community service that is curriculum based and directly connected to social justice, difference, and citizenship. The program at Hobart and William Smith Colleges (HWS) will provide illustrations of this type of work, although all service learning programs must engage certain universal issues if they honestly connect academic excellence, ethical education, and community responsibility.

Primary among these issues must be the development of a genuine partnership with the participating community organizations and neighborhoods. Anything less can easily atrophy into a coincidental if not exploitative relationship between the educational institution, the instructor's class, and the larger community. It easily may become just another example of institutional patriarchy, reducing those "in receipt" of the service to objects for academic study. To avoid such detours, community representatives must from the very beginning be brought into the dialogue about the course and the program. Most are delighted to be asked, and though wary at first, they find the enthusiasm of the students and the richness of the course content a refreshing resource for their own work. The more that participants appear in the classroom, and the more that faculty and the public service coordinator appear at the site, the greater the dialogue and trust that will develop between the community and college. The point is to find a thoughtful relationship between teacher, learner, subject matter, and community—one where the lines are somewhat blurred and where ideas, experience, and action mix to form a new type of learning.

As a means to ensure a genuine partnership, certain issues need to be addressed directly. One critical component is a thorough training program for students that outlines the historic and sociopolitical dynamics of the community. Along with faculty and community representatives, students need a broader understanding of the location of this work and how and why it takes its present form. The site itself is another important part of this training. Its particular history and context must be addressed, as well as its purpose and goals. Beyond this, an acceptable training program must include issues of personal responsibility, confidentiality, interpersonal relations, and some beginning introduction to the course and to the instructor's goals for the public service component. The fundamental point rests on equipping students adequately for community work, so that they may learn, grow, and contribute.

The administration of the training program requires a great amount of time and thought. A comprehensive service learning program necessitates that a full-time administrative college staff position be dedicated to this work. Usually the position falls under the title of coordinator or director of public service. Without adequate oversight and support, these programs run aground on the rocks of good intentions. Faculty alone need a great amount of logistical support in identifying partners and nurturing these relationships. Once students are placed at sites, it is incumbent on the coordinator to follow up with oversight and assessment, otherwise faculty will find themselves overwhelmed with a full menu of "in-field" problems ranging from student needs, transportation problems, site placement issues, and general follow-up with the community partners. A number of programs have augmented the coordinator's efforts with a host of peer educators, trained to perform many of these specific functions and usually drawn from the ranks of students concentrating in service learning and community work.

Two other fundamental issues remain. First, the degree of integration between the course and the service must be significant. Simply assigning service as an option or a requirement without centering it within the everyday dialogue of the classroom will so marginalize and disconnect it from the course content that it is most likely to become a parallel assignment for the students. It will most certainly fail to align ideas, experience, and action into the transformative, critical pedagogical experience it could become, and thus it is not likely to produce the sort of critical reflection the integrative model requires. Community-based learning requires significantly more intimacy between classroom and community, an intimacy that produces a "borderless classroom" with a wholly different complexion and where the assigned readings now include an experiential one—the community itself as text.

Finally, the instruction must be clear about the possible motives for involving students in community service. Sometimes these motives are represented as dualistic, setting altruism against political transformation. Put another way, many service programs must decide whether students are "serving" others as a form of charitable activity or participating in metapolitical work that aims to engage issues of powerlessness, social justice, and political and economic change. Much debate has ensued over these different orientations, ranging from the individualistic and virtue-centered writings of William Buckley (1990) and William Bennett (1993) to the more political approach taken by Benjamin Barber (1993) and Harry Boyte (1993). Buckley and Bennett emphasize service as just that—individual charitable acts of human decency—whereas Barber and Boyte understand the need for the political education of emerging citizens in a fragile democracy.

The type of community-based learning appropriate for a multi-centric democracy clearly embraces both the need to refine altruistic sensibilities and the existential foundations of participatory democracy. In many ways the dualism of the charitable instinct and the political impulse proves to be a false one. Robert Coles's formidable work *The Call of Service* (1993) captures the tension. In describing his involvement with the early civil rights movement, Coles relates the story of a young girl named Tessie, one of the four children who integrated the New Orleans school system in 1961. Struck by her calm in the face of a violent hurricane of white resistance and probable violence, Coles is overwhelmed by Tessie's conviction that her courageous act is really an act of service to others. The nine-year-old tells him that she puts her life at risk because she is "called" to it as part of God's will to see morality served. Her sense of religious commitment is joined to her innate sense of social justice. In Coles's words, "she had connected a civic moment in her life with a larger ideal, and in so doing had learned to regard herself as a servant, as a person 'called to service'" (p. 6). In this poignant tale, Coles helps us understand that public service retains the critical elements of human decency joined to civic connection. Ultimately, public service frames the range of values and commitment essential for a robust democratic citizenship.

Public Service at Hobart and William Smith Colleges

Service learning at Hobart and William Smith Colleges consists of an integrated curricular, co-curricular, and residential public service program. Much of it explicitly attempts to address issues of difference, community, and intercultural citizenship. The colleges, Hobart for men and William Smith for women, form one institution whose origins date from 1822. Located in Geneva, New York, the colleges are a private, liberal arts undergraduate institution with 1,750 students, the large majority of whom are housed in campus residences.

Geneva is a small rural city wedged between Syracuse and Rochester. The political economy of Geneva serves as a microcosm of social difference in urban America. Once thought to be the new western economic frontier for the emerging industrial system in the nineteenth century, Geneva now stands as vivid testimony to the brutal process of economic disinvestment and deindustrialization. Deserted by its once busy factories, its mostly Italian American population finds itself struggling to maintain its tight family and kinship culture.

Long preceding industrialization and the arrival of an imported European labor force in the last stages of the nineteenth century, Geneva from its earliest days served as home for a vibrant African American community. Nineteenth-century Virginian plantation owners built summer houses along the Seneca Lake shore and brought many of their slaves along. Soon Geneva became a conduit on the underground railroad, and throughout most of its history Geneva was home to a sizeable African American community.

In the twentieth century, further social change brought an increased black migration. Today Geneva's population comprises members of various European ethnic groups, African Americans, a growing Latino component, and an extensive white agrarian population. Geneva's class composition is equally segmented, including a dwindling working class, a not insignificant rural poor component, a sizeable immigrant labor population mostly tied to the wine vineyards and farming community, a longstanding upper class, and a professional and middle-class tier. Most of these different classes arrived during the various economic epochs illustrative of American history. Typical is its modern-day nomadic population found wandering the streets, dispossessed and out of the American economic mainstream.

As a highly segmented and, some would argue, segregated rural city, Geneva is remarkably diverse compared to the rest of upstate New York. It suffers, though, from its equally segmented economic system, which is bounded by the contradictions of the global postmodern system that devalues much of Geneva's history. Geneva witnesses the unrelenting decline of its industrial base and is unable to locate the roots of the upscale side of the new service economy. Its only growth appears to be in an endless expansion of low-paying, unsecured jobs attached to the low end of the retail service sector.

The colleges' public service program operates within this context of class hypersegmentation and economic eclipse. Long providing idiosyncratic volunteer opportunities for their students, the colleges more recently inaugurated a more intentional program of community-based learning. The American Commitments program offers a twenty-course curriculum and an expansive array of volunteer opportunities organized by the office of public service. The two principal student volunteer organizations are the Student Literacy Corps and Students Organized for Service. A full range of community partners maintains a close connection to the colleges. An on-campus residence is dedicated to public service. Its members help produce an on-campus public service newsletter, *Potential*. Finally, the campus and its community partners sponsor an annual day of service that attracts more than one thousand volunteers at approximately fifty local sites. It is followed by a community-campus picnic as an annual celebration of their joint partnership.

The American Commitments curriculum consists of courses across the spectrum, including political science, sociology, biology, mathematics, education, religious studies, chemistry, philosophy, economics, and African and Latino studies. Students in these courses work at community sites arranged by the coordinator for public service and the participating faculty member. The sites usually include the local hospital, schools, residential drug treatment centers, migrant worker literacy sites, the local Head Start program, the local food pantry, lunch programs for the needy and homeless, and other community and neighborhood organizations. In short, the mosaic of courses and community sites presents students and neighbors with a full array of ideas and experiences that tease out the issues of social difference, economic justice, and intercultural citizenship.

One such course is "Politics, Community, and Service." It offers us some deeper insights into the promise of community-based learning for addressing democracy, community, and difference. As it is a service learning course, students are required to be fully engaged in a term-long community service project. The course asks students to enter the biographies of people within the community and to be involved in writing autobiographically about the effect of that service on their own lives, their perspectives on democracy, and their understanding of democratic citizenship.

It is also a course that prizes independent thought. It focuses on the critical evaluation of both the readings and the field experience and of how each serves to illuminate the other. Students are asked to reaffirm one central precept, namely, that learning requires a serious commitment to both the subject at hand and the voices and experiences of those engaged in the course and the community.

Students are involved in community service from two perspectives. First, Geneva and its surroundings are a community in need of serious assistance as it encounters the limits, contradictions, and dramatic changes surrounding the realities of postmodern capitalism. Work in service involves students in the everyday lives of persons many times cornered by a very limited menu of social and economic choices. The experiences of Geneva residents and HWS students are authentic and real. The instructor works with them to enhance positive change in their immediate circumstances. This is the work of empowerment and social transformation.

Some of these students were fortunate to experience this form of social change directly. Several students revitalized the efforts of the local literacy program, working with individuals and families. Some of this involved work with migrant workers in the local wineries and vineyards. Literacy work was completed in both Spanish and English. By addressing both adults and children, literacy efforts had a profound impact on personal self-esteem, individual competency, and collective initiative in addressing the needs of a migrant population that is marginalized socially, politically, and economically.

Second, service work is in itself a project in citizenship. It explores the nature and limits of democratic citizenship in our time. This component of service learning is an essential and quite important commitment in its own right. What does citizenship mean now? What ought it mean? How does it relate to various perspectives on justice? Democracy? Community? Difference? Service learning ideally allows us to rethink these basic and critical concepts.

From both service learning perspectives (social change and democratic citizenship), students need to bring together experience and reason. Experience and ideas are ways to know the world, and our goal is to create a pedagogy—a way to learn—that joins the course readings with our field experience so that students can use each to understand and critically evaluate the other. Toward this end, the course attempts to end the narrow approach to education that separates learning from experience. That approach limits learning simply to the acquisition and absorption of knowledge. The course aims to end the equally false dualism of separating knowledge from personal experience. The goal of this course is to reconcile these different realms of learning by joining readings and experience, intellectual development and ethical growth, and the individual academic experience with the unfolding student autobiographies.

Writing, Reading, and Doing:
The Journal, the Ethnography, the Autobiography

In "Politics, Community, and Service," each student must regularly use a dialogical experiential journal. The journal is composed of three sections. Students are required to write insightful and reflective reviews (not reports) of what they find to be key aspects of the assigned readings. In addition, they write about their field experience in some detail, but they also compare that experience to the readings. What do their experience and the readings have in common and how do they differ? Students read each other's journals so that they can share their ideas and experiences.

In addition, students are asked to write two analytic argumentative papers in which they critically evaluate much of the course readings and the central arguments of the assigned authors. But two additional assignments, together with several required submissions of the journal for review, further integrate the course readings with the field experience. One of these assignments is a required ethnographic portrait of a community person encountered in the field work. In this writing, students are asked to be intelligent observers as well as participants in the community. They meet persons whose lives tell stories about one or more key aspects of community life: class, ethnic, racial, gender, and other forms of social difference, political empowerment, or political powerlessness. Students encounter the circumstances of material shortcomings, economic jeopardy, and the anxieties brought on by semipermanent economic vulnerability; they hear stories of great courage in overcoming seemingly insurmountable obstacles. In this assignment, students grasp that they too are authors with important insights into the personal stories of another significant person. The assigned works from Robert Coles's *The Call of Service* (1993), Studs Terkel's *Race* (1992), Gloria Anzaldua's *Borderlands/La Frontera* (1987), and

Audre Lorde's *Sister Outsider* (1984) prove excellent sources for this work.

The final written assignment is an intellectual and ethical citizen autobiography. Students are explicitly asked to reflect on their experience with the authors, the course discussions, and their community involvement in such a way that the experience becomes a "text" in itself, a text to be engaged, assessed, and evaluated. Students are asked, "How has the class helped you reexamine your personal, ethical, and political values? What does service learning mean for your understanding of democratic citizenship?" In short, they are asked to articulate what they believe, what they do, and what they have read. By joining action to knowledge and reflection, students consciously become the subjects of democracy, political actors in and around a community in which they are intimately involved. In the moments of the course experience, they are developing the democratic imagination and personal commitments required of an active citizen.

One poignant example is that of a young student, Kristina, whose voice we hear later in this chapter. She was working with a local food group distributing groceries to low-income individuals and families. She wrote extensively in her journal and for her citizen autobiography about her intense feelings of guilt and her privileged position in society in contradistinction to the plight of the people with whom she worked alongside. She came from a middle-income family in New England, a family of liberal viewpoints and keen sensitivity to the needs of others. Still, she experienced deep anxiety about her own feelings of social distance and privilege. Ultimately she came to the realization that society placed "borders," as she put it, around all social differences and that these borders were largely irrelevant on a personal basis. She wrote about her realization of how the "self-other" dichotomy is a socially created construct. With that insight, she is now capable of sustaining a full commitment to social activism and personal involvement regardless of the uneasiness of the social setting. She has learned that the disquieting aspect of traversing class difference is an artificial barrier to human connection. This was a remarkable existential break-through, aided by the conjunction of the readings, the field work, and the writing.

Field Work

As previously discussed, students in the "Politics, Community, and Service" course engaged in a wide variety of community projects ranging from literacy work and volunteering in the local food pantry to active work with the rape crisis center and "neighbor-hood watch" associations. On average, students worked between three to five hours per week over a ten-week term. The Hobart and William Smith office of public service helped with placements, field assessment, and overall logistical support.

Individual student experience varied at the different sites. Some students had major encounters with their own value systems, whereas others had rather routine involvement with the agencies. One young woman working with a women's organization con-fronted issues of sexual abuse that resonated with her own personal experience. Her dialogical journal represented deep reflection about the readings, particularly those discussing issues of gender and difference as well as those analyzing conditions of empower-ment. Although her field experience was deeply personal, it was not very qualitatively different from that of many of the students. Almost everything related to reflective discussions about issues of equity, justice, and care. For most of the students, this class was their first opportunity to frame their community work in a larger context of rigorous intellectual work and group reflection.

Other students encountered firsthand some of the fundamen-tal social barriers to ethnic and racial harmony within the commu-nity. Working with neighborhood improvement groups, they witnessed the deep-seated racial antagonism that surrounds such issues as the inclusion of low-income tenants, usually Latino or African American, in neighborhood efforts aimed at anticrime campaigns. To some of the more economically secure residents, welfare recipients and low-income groups *were* the problem they wanted to solve. They viewed single-parent, poor families as spawning grounds for crime and neighborhood decay. Students came to these issues more as naive initiates, and at first were bewildered about how to engage the obvious biases. After a time, they would gently but forthrightly state their position of wanting to help everyone in the neighborhood and to create bridges where possible. The depth of racial and class divisions became very real to the students; most students increased their determination to engage those divisions as effectively as possible. This attitude is in stark contrast to that of many of these students' uninvolved college associates who remain largely unaware or indifferent to the omnipresent nature of such social conflicts, and accordingly see politics as something remote from their personal lives.

Student Voices

What follows are the voices of four students from three different offerings of the "Politics, Community, and Service" course. Each represents many of the issues surrounding intercultural citizenship discussed in this chapter.

Valerie

Valerie is from the South Bronx, New York. She is a Latina student who is struggling to become an accomplished young woman while retaining her allegiance to her home community and cultural heritage. These passages are drawn from her "citizenship autobiography." She volunteered at Hannick Hall, a residential drug treatment center housing only women, mostly young mothers from New York City, Albany, Buffalo, Rochester, and Syracuse. All are recovering crack addicts, and Hannick is set up to house them and their children. Valerie found that in her community service and in the course readings she was at the border between her two worlds. Here she struggles for a vocabulary of citizenship and social justice that will provide her an affirmative identity and civic work. She left Geneva and the colleges for two terms after her participation in this class. She is still struggling to connect her separate worlds.

Four chairs and an ashtray. That is all that occupied the patio of Hannick Hall. Four chairs and an ashtray, at one time, was the key that opened a door within myself. How was I to know that at Hannick Hall, I would find a piece of myself. A piece I too, like all of the Hannick Hall women, had once lost. On a Thursday evening after dinner I took notice of a very important issue. Lydia, Andrea, Sharon and myself were all sitting, smoking and sharing the comfort of silence in a world of thunder. I thought for a moment that it was my place as the volunteer to try to get to know the mindframe that makes Hannick Hall. Little did I know, I already did. Four women, four chairs and four different roads travelled. All meeting under a moonlit night at a rehabilitation center, where we had the opportunity to look into a mirror and see inside ourselves. What had led us to believe that in the comfort of strangers was where we could find ourselves? Could it have been our similarities? All of us representing the "minority." Two Puerto Rican and two African American. Or the fact that we all were raised in an inner city, and that our only access to a decent education was the N.Y. City public school system, where today metal detectors are needed to keep order and safety in the school. Well whatever it was that allowed us to bond was definitely appreciated. All three of these women were alcoholics, drug addicts, prostitutes and even drug dealers. Hannick Hall was their mecca. It's the place where women go when they have had their final high, a place where they come to receive light after death. In my eyes Hannick Hall housed women rejected by society, full of pain, tears and dreams [deferred].

My placement there was full of irony. In each of those strong women, I saw myself. In Andrea's eyes I saw her six children being born with drug addictions to heroin, cocaine and/or crack. I also saw my neighbors' children, suffering from malnourishment. In Sharon's eyes, I saw the pain of an abused mother of one. I saw every child's mom at the neighborhood children's center. In Lydia's eyes, I saw much more. I saw the attitude that is taught by Latina mothers to their daughters. In that attitude exists a whole other person. It's what helps us survive in the inner city. The attitude of, "I am my only provider, and I will survive." Through the service at Hannick Hall and our class, I learned that a community can do a great deal of good if used effectively. The three women I referred to are very strong and determined to put the past behind them. Although they have Hannick Hall, it will take them a long time to get over the poverty, hunger and substance abuse. The government supplies communities in need with programs that help ease the tensions of poverty and poor education. After all the two are linked. In communities such as mine, there is a great need for service, but it is in my opinion that anyone can do service. Not everyone can be impressionable. Robert Coles often referred to instances where he witnessed the malleable attitudes that society portrayed towards the "minority." In the case of my community everyone is a "minority" and cannot be reached by people who are new to the "game."

As I look at how my role in each of the following communities has changed I can't help but to ask, why? Why is it that as a student in Geneva I was a leader of the "minority" community, proud president of the Latin American Organization, assistant manager of the revived Third World Cultural Center, and Latina spokesperson for Una Umoja Juyey [themed residence]. In this particular community my greatest enemy was the ignorance of my peers. As a volunteer at Hannick Hall, I was the cool volunteer who was easy to approach, and very seclusive about where I was from. In the South Bronx, I am a completely different person. In fact, I've become invisible. And what has become visible to me, are the awful living conditions my people in my community, as well as myself, are forced to live under.

Being away from Geneva has taught me much. It also allowed me to analyze America's great democracy. What is democracy? A question our class has pondered on many occasions. Well, I believe democracy is a people's government. Is it? At 721 Linton Avenue in the Bronx does democracy exist? Let's see . . . four housing projects on every block of fifteen floors each. Ten apartments on each floor. Two elevators hazardous to our health. A stairwell painted with a paint that was supposed to be fireproof. Maybe, but it's also dangerous for asthmatics to be around, due to the fumes of the paint, which still exist two months after the paint was applied. These are merely conditions inside the building and not those outside in the street. I guess for the Latino and African "Americans" of this community democracy does not exist.

Living in these conditions often allowed me to analyze the concept of community. It is in my belief that if members of "inner city" communities were affluent or educated, then perhaps the imbalance of education, experience, living conditions, etc. would have to leave. Who do you think it will be?

I know that communities in suburbs have problems but in suburbs there is a balance in the community. All members (citizens) have decent educations, jobs, and connections. Therefore if one is needy they can be referred to another for help. In communities such as mine, who refers to whom? Crack addicts refer prostitutes to crack spots, or the drug spots. Other than that, not much goes on in my community. All this leads me to the question of, what is citizenship? Citizenship is who one *is*, a virtue of what one believes in, what one does, and what one has learned. Citizenship to me has changed, and will continue to evolve as my perspective communities are involved and change. In Geneva, I had great responsibilities to my community. Has that changed now that I am a citizen of the Bronx? It shouldn't, but it has. My community has to want help. Otherwise it will not honor it. My community service today is working with high school students, teaching and counseling them through a government funded program called College Bound. And I am grateful to the course I took, the professor I took it with, for allowing me the opportunity to see within myself and make the necessary arrangements I needed. My place is to be here in my community where I'm needed. Too many young children are following the arrows that point them in the direction to Hannick Hall. I just can't watch it happen and ignore it anymore.

Vanessa

Vanessa is a white, middle-class young woman from Philadelphia. She graduated shortly after this class, and she is now completing a law degree at an excellent law school. She hopes to use her degree to fashion a legal career around social justice. In "Politics, Community, and Service" she volunteered at the local mediation board. She first went through thirty-plus hours of mandatory training before she was a certified mediator. Her experience gave her great pause about her understanding of the economic, political, and social issues surrounding the nation at the close of this century. The piece that follows is drawn from Vanessa's ethnographic portrait of a young boy whose mother was part of a mediation Vanessa was observing. She crosses a wide chasm of race and class.

One of the most gratifying sentiments found in the expansive spectrum of human emotion is one of interconnected identification: the simple feeling that you are not alone in this life, that you indeed make up a small part of an integrated whole. When you realize that other people share the same feelings and experiences as you, you realize that these similarities form a cohesive bond strong enough to overcome both your apparent and actual differences. Such was my realization one week ago as an observer in an assault mediation. I never thought that a little black boy and his young mother would change from victims of society into mirrors in which I saw crucial elements of myself. The prevalent paradox of community service arose that day both in my being and experience; namely the unexpected transformation in which the recipients of service became the givers and the giver of service became the receiver. I learned from their characters and circumstances first-hand about human similarities and how those similarities overcome and outshine human differences. The little black boy and his mother were living affirmations who proved to me the inherent human interconnectedness that secures us together in the circle of life. Upon first glance it was the differences between this little boy, his mother and myself that seemed most apparent. We appeared to be separated by the vast gulfs of our race, class and education. Race was the first difference that caught my attention, as it is the easiest to detect. I walked down the hall of a former school towards the mediation office. As the heels of my shoes clicked and echoed in the empty hallway, suddenly I heard a jarring thump sound that I knew didn't come from my feet. I came upon a little black boy sitting on his chubby, young mother's lap looking up at me with the perplexed look children often have when they are deciding whether to cry or laugh after injuring themselves. I realized he had hit his head on the wall and knew from years of experience with children that if I could make him laugh, give him comfort that he was all right, he could be deterred from crying. "Wow, you really knocked your coconut on the wall, I'm surprised you didn't crack the wall open!" I said laughing, watching his face, as well as his mother's, transform from apprehension, to surprise, to laughter. Looking at their somewhat unkempt appearances and knowing they were here for a biracial assault mediation, I formed personal presuppositions of how their race, class, and education separated our experiences. I hypothesized that the mother was a single, welfare recipient, uneducated and generally mistrusting of white people.

As I began to wrestle with the meaning and ramifications of my personal ideological metamorphosis and my newfound conviction in the necessity of communal participation, essays like *Habits of the Heart* by Robert Bellah confirmed my convictions and comforted my confusion. I counted myself among the "many of those" Bellah spoke with who "were locked into a split between a public world of competitive striving and a private world supposed to provide the meaning and love that make competitive striving bearable" (Bellah [and others, 1985], p. 115). "Learning by doing" unlocked the split into which my conservative upbringing locked me. I found that it was community service that could provide "the meaning and love that make competitive striving bearable" and justifiable. Through working through various disputes with a variety of people, I started to suspect that communal participation was not only necessary to substantiate personal morale but also societal morale. Bellah's essay confirmed my suspicions. His argument that in "reconstituting the social world, personal transformation among large numbers is essential . . . [but] it must not only be a transformation of consciousness . . . it must also involve individual action" (p. 111) helped me to intellectually identify the insinuations of my service. I now knew why I began to think that not only did I need to change my views, but also my actions; it was a necessary process in "reconstituting the social world," the community of which I am a part. Bellah's writing showed me that my credo conflict is both explicatable and crucial to civic maturation.

As the class and my service progressed, my conviction that community service is a vital component of democratic citizenship grew stronger. After having reached this conclusion, I started to think about my future and how this conclusion would affect and shape it. I had spent the summer working with a cutthroat, successful, expensive attorney who specialized in litigation. I thought I would follow his career course: Penn Law School, a judicial clerkship, three or four years in the DA's office, and then start on the ladder leading to senior partnership. I thought this was what I wanted to and would do. Working at the Center for Dispute Settlement made this plan impossible. Seeing how much greater the need was for legal assistance in resolution (rather than prolongment, as the case is with litigation) awoke my sleeping conscience.

Perhaps one of the most important revelations I've had about democratic citizenship as a result of this class is that it "is based upon the conviction that there are extraordinary possibilities in ordinary people" (Harry Emerson Fosdick). Through all of the readings and my service, I discovered the extraordinary possibilities within myself. This discovery led to my departure from civic and communal disconnection and [my] dedication to civic and communal connection. Although this redefinition of self was frightening and frustrating, as it seemed to rob me of stability and certainty, I, like Lorde, "began to recognize a source of power within myself that comes from the knowledge that while it is most desirable not to be afraid, learning to put fear into a perspective gave me great strength" (Lorde, [1984,] p. 41). I will use this strength to bring forth and act on the extraordinary possibilities within me throughout the remainder of my life.

Kristina

Kristina grew up in a small community in rural Maine. She is quiet and reserved by nature. She volunteered at the local food pantry while enrolled in "Politics, Community, and Service." Working in the community and with the course readings brought her into a world of conflict around class and race differences that was outside of her more traditional and idealistic upbringing. This short excerpt from one of her analytic essays on the readings is joined to another excerpt from her "citizenship autobiography."

Through this course I have developed an appreciation for the values that have been instilled in me, as well as for the many influences in my life that served to instill them. My experiences at the Food Pantry have brought the class readings to life and helped me to see how, despite my values, society has still managed to infiltrate into my life and my perceptions of people.

I found that, even though I knew that all people deserve to be treated equally, to have equal opportunities in life, and to be respected and valued for their varying, yet equal contributions to society, I had trouble overcoming the stereotypes and fears dictated by society about poor people. I had, without realizing it, internalized these stereotypes so that they affected my perceptions of these people. I realize now that the anxiety and guilt I felt on that first day at the Food Pantry was a result of the fact that, deep down, I was being forced to recognize and confront my fear that I would be blamed for the living conditions of these people who I did not even know. When, to my surprise, I was accepted without judgment by the majority of the people I met at the Food Pantry, I was able to let go of my guilt and fear enough to accept and engage our differences, thus bridging the gap between us. This is the very same process that Audre Lorde describes in her book, *Sister Outsider*.

Like Robert Coles, I have come to appreciate the insights these people are able to provide into the problems of society. They have also helped me to view my own life in relation to the larger society. Because of the present structure of our society, those who are at the bottom are not afforded the same opportunities for participation in the creation of our society. They are not treated as valid citizens with valuable insights and experiences to add to the process of naming and renaming the very communities in which they live. Also, the people at the top don't tend to see the connection between their personal gain and the resulting loss of others. This loss of connectedness, on both ends of the spectrum, has resulted in a loss of community and, with it, the values of mutual respect, unconditional acceptance, love, cooperation and compromise, all of which benefit the whole, rather than the privileged few.

Through this class, I have been made painstakingly aware of the boundaries that I have allowed, whether through ignorance or fear, to exist in my own life. The authors we have read have helped me to understand how those boundaries came into being and, in doing so, have provided me with means to dissolve such boundaries as I come across them in the course of my life. Boundaries serve no purpose other than to keep people separated so that they do not have to see how their everyday actions and decisions necessarily impact on others. In creating and maintaining boundaries, we are supporting a society that allows its members to suffer and die on a daily basis, while the rest of us are busy competing to see who can get into the best school, have the highest paying job, and drive the shiniest car. If we were to glance across the barriers we have created, we would have to confront the death and destruction we are perpetuating on the other side and be forced to give up our way of life. If we do not bother to glance over, we continue to support values that strip us all of our humanity. We spend our lives working to gain material wealth and the power and prestige that comes with it. Yet, in our quest to get ahead, we abuse friendships and break family ties, and when it comes time to sit back and enjoy the material wealth we have spent our lives acquiring, we find that we have no one left to share it with. Without anyone to share it with, it is meaningless. Through community service, or through the sharing of life with others on a day-to-day basis, everyone benefits.

Jeremy

Jeremy is a remarkable undergraduate. He is a pre-med biology major. Since his first year in college he has been volunteering in the local hospital's emergency room, as an ambulance EMT, and as an elected leader on campus. He is a resident assistant in the dorms, an honors student, and a genuine campus leader. He enrolled in "Politics, Community, and Service" and volunteered as an EMT. He wrote extensively about those aspects of the course that were new to him—issues of social difference, particularly race, and issues of citizenship education. He grew up in an upper-middle-class suburban neighborhood, most recently in Maryland. He will attend medical school and pursue a career in medicine.

It is often argued that Americans today do not know what citizenship really means. Scapegoats for community problems abound, and we constantly expect the government to do something about the problems that face us as a nation. We demand that our leaders show us the way through hard times, and that they alone rebuild our country. Cornel West once mentioned that, "we are constantly scapegoating . . . the result . . . the erosion of personal morality and self respect" (lecture). What West is getting at is that we no longer have a sense of what citizenship really means. We find it easier to put the blame on someone else rather than tackle the problem ourselves. A definition of citizenship offered by the dictionary is, "The character of an individual viewed as a member of society." Superficially, this says nothing about personal morality, self respect, or dedication to one's community. However, if one looks at the relationship of an individual as a member of society, we realize that to be a citizen one must *participate* in that society. For without individual participation, we would not be living in a democracy. The question then remains: How do we learn to be citizens and participate in our democratic community?

Experience in service learning is essential in the education process toward becoming learned citizens. A vital part of our education, service teaches individuals how to work together for a common goal. Whether that goal is simply painting a fence, working with hospital patients, or feeding the hungry, it causes all involved persons to put aside their differences, and act as true citizens participating in their community. Service coerces persons to take a look at their community and become involved in the changes that happen there. Farland and Henry mention, "isolation from the larger world is the principle obstacle to education for public life." It is this involvement in service that creates pride and a sense of responsibility in one's community. For it is when members of the community take responsibility for their environment, that they truly become citizens. They have the character traits—honor, pride and responsibility, among others—that define them as true citizens of society.

Conclusion

These eloquent and passionate student voices most effectively demonstrate the power of community-based learning as a pedagogy for evoking the interplay of difference, community, and intercultural citizenship. Community-based learning allows for those teachable moments that forge experience, ideas, and autobiography into one conversation about values and action. And at this intersection, community-based learning sets in motion the democratic imagination. It helps demystify the "self-other" dichotomy that serves as a cornerstone of social stereotypes and cultural ignorance. Service learning allows students to cross borders closed to them in the normal course of curricular and campus life. In addition, service learning begins to restore the ideal of community and community life. To many students, life in the overly privatized and disconnected suburbs, or the fragmentation of the inner city, has left them with radical skepticism about the possibilities of community. In the wake of collapsing community organizations—churches, neighborhood organizations, civic groups, and extended family systems—the very possibility of an extended system of human interdependence appears remote, if not naive. Service learning helps to restore faith in the experience of human interconnection and community life.

Service learning rebuilds a belief in the efficacy of individual action and community participation. The voices of these students testify to the affirmation of personal responsibility as a central feature in their service experience. In a period of political cynicism, many students are drawn to service work as a new way to involve themselves in political and community life with the hope of making a palpable difference in the private and public worlds surrounding these communities.

But most important of all, service learning introduces students to a most essential feature of democratic citizenship, namely, the revaluing of public life and the veneration of public life's civic domain. There is no participatory democracy without a vibrant civil society. This must include all those civic experiences that introduce young people to those private arenas where human decency is prized. A democracy without a moral and ethical foundation—and the organizations that nurture and protect it—can only be at best a majoritarian political mechanism. And although some democratic theorists may contend that this is the best we can expect in a postmodern global economy, many students are affirming that an older classical ideal of civic virtue is alive and well. That older ideal can now be joined to a multicultural and intercultural historical moment. Service learning can itself "serve" to restore citizenship education in an age of difference and intercultural conflict.

Chapter Three

Finding Community Across Boundaries

Service Learning in Women's Studies

Mary K. Trigg, Barbara J. Balliet

A central idea behind the national impetus toward placing service learning in the curriculum is the belief that it teaches college students what it means to be citizens in a democratic society. This concept emphasizes service as the responsibility of citizenship and argues that an educated and engaged citizenry is a prerequisite for a healthy democracy (Barber and Battistoni, 1993). Advocates of service learning hope it will contribute to the creation of new generations of citizens who understand the way government works and who will feel and act on their sense of responsibility to their communities.

Women's studies is a particularly useful field from which to explore the contribution service learning can make to American collegiate education. Women's studies has a double identity within the university. Programs seek to include their subject—women—in the traditional curriculum while also recognizing the need for a separate location to develop new methods of inquiry that more fully explore the historical and contemporary position of women in society. The position of women's studies as an outsider *within* the academy parallels the position of students as they enter communities from the university as part of service education courses

(Collins, 1986; Harding, 1991). Even when students share ethnic, racial, and class identities with members of the communities in which they work, their purpose as learners differentiates them. Students in service learning courses are charged with empowering others while they use their experiences as a route to empowering themselves. Similarly, women's studies faculty are engaged in transforming knowledge and questioning institutional power and hierarchy while benefiting from their position within the academy.

In service learning, students learn across boundaries as they move between communities and classrooms. In feminist service learning courses, this movement occurs primarily in and among communities of women. Gender provides a special lens on the social issues students encounter in both their placements and readings. For example, students learn that poverty affects men and women differently. Ideas about community, hierarchy, and identity are experienced and critically examined in a context that puts gender at the center of analysis.

Women students need to learn about American women's long and rich tradition of volunteering in their communities (Frankel and Dye, 1991; Ginzberg, 1991). The complicated history of women's community activism helps students forge an understanding of *their* location in this history and of the different possibilities for female citizenship. The history of women's voluntarism also demonstrates the problems that can arise when women cross class, racial, and ethnic boundaries in the name of service, democracy, or sisterhood. Historically, voluntarism and community building offered some women an avenue for gaining self-confidence, and were socially acceptable ways to develop leadership and political skills working with communities of less privileged women. Women students today can study women's history to reflect on ways, both positive and negative, in which their voluntarism might affect the lives of those they serve in the community. Through community service, they can gain a growing recognition of themselves as women and as citizen leaders.

Women's Studies at Rutgers University

Rutgers University, the state university of New Jersey, is a residential public research and undergraduate university. A large and at times impersonal institution, Rutgers enrolls about forty thousand students and has campuses in Newark, Camden, and New Brunswick. There are eight undergraduate colleges scattered across New Brunswick and Piscataway. The Rutgers student body is ethnically and racially diverse, and the majority of Rutgers undergraduates come from New Jersey. Most Rutgers students are from working-class and middle-class family backgrounds; many of them are the first persons in their families to have attended college (Moffat, 1989).

The women's studies program at Rutgers was founded in 1971 as an interdisciplinary certificate program. It became an interdisciplinary major in 1984. As one of the oldest of the more than six hundred women's studies programs currently in existence in the United States, its form and its challenges cannot be detached from the movements that helped to create it—the civil rights movement and the second-wave feminist movement. (DuBois and others, 1987; Aisenberg and Harrington, 1988; Schuster and Van Dyne, 1985). Women's studies remains shaped by its history, created in the years after black and ethnic studies had arrived on college campuses. Like most early programs, women's studies at Rutgers was originally molded by the passion (and largely volunteer labor) of women faculty. They discovered through the women's movement the androcentric bias of most of the traditional curriculum and resolved to reconstruct knowledge by describing and analyzing women's experiences. A proposal drafted in 1973 by a group of women faculty urging the establishment of a women's studies program at Rutgers defined the enterprise as a "center for research and teaching about women within the university" and as an "academic field concerned with the history, accomplishments, roles, status and attributes of women; and with sex roles in American society and other cultures" (Milstein, 1993, p. 14).

The program's beginnings in feminist politics and scholarship have left an indelible print on the curriculum and on the program's relationship to the university. Faculty and students in the program struggle over the relationships between feminist theory and practice, advocacy and scholarship, and how much women's studies should emulate other academic departments and disciplines. Women's studies is valued by both faculty and students for its putting gender on the academic map as a social and intellectual category, for its critique of institutional hierarchy and inequality, for its openness to interdisciplinary scholarship, and as a site of intellectual experimentation and camaraderie.

The History of Women's Studies

These values, core to women's studies, represent a significant challenge to business as usual within the academy. Feminist scholarship and pedagogy reevaluate how knowledge is produced, stressing partnership and active participation in the classroom over competition and rote learning. Founded in absence—the absence of women from the traditional curriculum—women's studies fosters a critical perspective, examining the disciplines carefully for androcentrism and stressing the inseparability of gender from other social categories, such as race, ethnicity, and sexuality. Women's studies was created in a context where disciplines organized in the late nineteenth and early twentieth centuries claimed to represent objective knowledge but had manifestly ignored how gender, class, race, and sexuality shaped the knowledge they produced. This latter insight, central to feminist scholarship, remains a tension both within women's studies and between women's studies and older disciplines. Feminists, in their effort to recover and analyze the experiences of women and to reconstruct knowledge, began trespassing on disciplinary boundaries, borrowing methods and theories from other disciplines.

This epistemological challenge again owes much to the early history of women's studies. Faculty from different disciplines brought together by a mutual interest in feminism and their status as women in the academy, frequently facing hostility within their departments, began to build interdisciplinary networks and to teach cross-disciplinary courses. Faculty in different departments anxious to transform their disciplines offered such courses as "Women and Literature," "Sociology of Gender," "Psychology of Women," and "Women and Work." Women's studies developed its curriculum using both new courses developed within traditional areas of study and the interdisciplinary, explicitly feminist courses. This dual impulse to transform disciplines through the inclusion of women and gender perspectives and to create a separate arena for the study of women and gender continues to shape women's studies (DuBois and others, 1987; Minnich, O'Barr, and Rosenfeld, 1988; Schuster and Van Dyne, 1985).

Feminist Pedagogy and Service Learning

The seminar that accompanies the women's studies community service experience at Rutgers is entitled "Community Activism: Women's Participation." It was inaugurated in fall 1992. Students receive a total of six credits: three for the seminar and three for ten to twelve hours of work at their site per week. The syllabus includes readings on feminist theory, which range from John Stuart Mill's *The Subjection of Women* to Diana M. Pearce's "The Feminization of Poverty," to bell hooks's *Feminist Theory: From Margin to Center*. It also includes readings on the history of women's community service and activism. Jane Addams's *Twenty Years at Hull House* is read alongside Ida B. Wells's *Struggle for Justice*. Students keep a journal in which they chronicle their daily experiences at their community sites and critically reflect on the connections or disjunctures between the feminist theories they are reading and the lives of the women with whom they are working. They also write a final paper in which they are asked to consider praxis, reframing their experiences using feminist theories.

The educational philosophy that shapes the course and serves as a framing idea for the program itself is drawn from feminist pedagogy. As it has developed over the last twenty-five years—often in tandem with women's studies programs throughout the country—feminist pedagogy has argued that the processes of learning and teaching should be reconceptualized (Culley and Portuges, 1985; Gabriel and Smithson, 1991; Griffin, 1993; Pagano, 1990). Feminist teaching methods stress collaboration over competition, legitimize personal experience as an appropriate arena of intellectual inquiry, and raise questions about the authority of the instructor. Feminist pedagogy strives to be nonhierarchical; that is, it emphasizes interpreting knowledge rather than simply acquiring it, and promotes student respect for one another and for the differing experiences and beliefs each student brings into the classroom. It strives to help students find, and use, their voices. In *Teaching to Transgress* (1994), bell hooks describes feminist pedagogy as "an alternative paradigm for teaching" that has "emphasized the issue of coming to voice." She writes: "That focus emerged as central, precisely because it was so evident that race, sex, and class privilege empower some students more than others, granting 'authority' to some voices more than others" (p. 185).

Feminist pedagogy has something valuable to offer to service learning courses. At its best, feminist pedagogy prepares students to reach out to community members with empathy and care. Participation in community service, like feminist pedagogy at an earlier point, has been hailed as a potentially transformative educational experience for undergraduates (Guarasci and Cornwell, 1993). In community service, students learn to engage in dialogue with community residents, share personal histories and experiences, and respect differences. Effective community service is collaborative, nonhierarchical, nonjudgmental, respectful, and transformative, embracing the same goals as effective feminist teaching methods. It encourages students to consider the notion of community itself, and how people form and sustain communities. In a similar spirit, the feminist classroom empowers students to think of themselves as members of a community and to interact in ways that will stimulate shared learning and mutual respect. Both ways of learning may motivate students to create new definitions of leadership, definitions that stress collective action rather than individualism and that suggest everyone can and should be a leader.

The women's studies internship program at Rutgers views service learning as an educational tool for our students, and approaches the community as a partner in education rather than as a set of clients in need of service. The same nonhierarchical, respectful, and nonjudgmental attitude that the feminist teacher fosters in the classroom should be the one that students take from the university out into the community with them. This approach encourages mutuality and seeks to avoid a charity-oriented, noblesse oblige philosophy. This approach not only helps to tear down the walls that often separate the university and the community in which it resides but also prepares students to enter a world in which the ability to reach across differences will be increasingly necessary.

Community Service at Rutgers

An internship experience has been a part of the women's studies curriculum at Rutgers since 1973, reflecting its feminist commitment to linking theory and practice and the academy to the community. A seminar, "Women and Contemporary Problems," was designed around community service to meet a program goal of combining scholarship with social involvement. During the late seventies the program shifted its focus, downplaying community activism in favor of career preparation. Students resisted this move, arguing for the creation of a one-credit course in which they could actively participate in "a particular political experience" that could be "analyzed in relation to theoretical material studied in class" (Orenstein, 1976–77, p. 7). By the mid-eighties, internships had again become a site for student initiative and experimentation. In 1992, under the auspices of the Rutgers Citizenship Education and Civic Leadership program (now Citizenship and Service Education), the internship became a course, adding a reading and writing curriculum, an instructor, and classroom experience.

The current women's studies internship program at Rutgers operates under the umbrella of the university-wide Citizenship and Service Education (CASE) program. This experiment in civic education and community service was launched at Rutgers in spring 1988, when President Edward Bloustein gave a commencement address in which he proposed a mandatory program of community service as a graduation requirement for all Rutgers students. His address called attention to the "pathologies of prejudice and radical individualism" manifest both in the nation and at Rutgers University (Barber and Battistoni, 1993, p. 235). He suggested the service requirement in response to what he perceived as a lack of connection and communication between the academic and local communities, the lives of students and their lives as citizens.

In 1990 the CASE program began to offer pilot courses integrating student community service into courses that were part of disciplinary majors. CASE is administered by the office of the vice-president for undergraduate education; it is directed by a full-time faculty member, and a staff member serves as an associate director. The program's larger goal is to link academic disciplines to general themes of community and citizenship through student service (Goldberg, 1992). The success of the pilot program was recognized by President Clinton when he chose Rutgers as the site to kick off his national service campaign in March 1993.

The Rutgers program currently offers more than a dozen courses that combine community service with classroom learning. The participating disciplines range from the social sciences (political science, psychology, and sociology) to such humanities disciplines as English, French, Spanish, and Portuguese, and include interdisciplinary programs, such as urban studies and women's studies. Although the intent is for each course to include the "core" civic education framework—which includes required readings and writing assignments on such topics as citizenship, diversity, and democracy—each course is adapted to the disciplinary concerns of the departments and programs that offer it. For example, a course cross-listed in political science and biology takes as its topic HIV and public policy, and offers students the opportunity to consider questions of public health, policy options, and social responsibility as they relate to issues surrounding HIV/AIDS. Students work in HIV-related community service placements, such as in a hospital pediatric AIDS ward or by delivering meals to people with AIDS (Barber and Battistoni, 1993).

From Feminist Theory to Practice

A community service course taught within the context of a women's studies program offers a means for students to move from feminist theory to practice. This is fueled by the idea that it's not enough to study feminist theory and writings in the classroom: the real goal is to improve women's lives. Students in a holistic learning experience like this one become practitioners of what they believe, or they recognize that for them, putting their theory into practice is an impossible task. A community service course can give students the opportunity to test, in a practical way, the kinds of classroom knowledge they may feel they have already learned. Striving for praxis is an advanced skill that may challenge the ways in which undergraduates have learned and the assumptions that they bring to their learning. This pedagogy is rooted in a history of educational theory developed most prominently by John Dewey (1957), a theory that combines intellectual life with public citizenship. Service learning courses provide a broader context through readings and discussion of the experiences students are having in the community. As one of our students wrote about her service with a transitional home for formerly homeless women:

"My eyes were opened, unlike they could have been in any other way, to the circumstances that poor women are faced with. I was never before aware of how few of the needs of women in poverty are actually met by our 'welfare' system."

To understand more fully the unique problems of the women whom they serve in the community, students need to be taught, through feminist writings, the legacy of institutional sexism in the United States and the impact that economic discrimination and exclusion from political participation have had on women's lives. It is also necessary that they learn the ways in which institutionalized racism has compounded these difficulties for women of color. The challenges faced by poor women, for example, who may be burdened with single motherhood along with wage discrimination, are different from the challenges faced by poor men. When confronted with real women with real problems, the women's studies student can begin to understand and use feminist theories as tools for improving women's condition rather than as abstract sets of ideas.

Most of the community sites at which students from the Rutgers women's studies program volunteer focus on problems in which gender plays a defining role. The placements include Planned Parenthood offices, women's health and counseling centers, rape crisis centers, battered women's shelters, a transitional home for formerly homeless women, and a YWCA project for pregnant teenagers. Many of these organizations are primarily or exclusively female environments. One reflection of the program's success is the relatively high percentage of students who choose to continue volunteering after their internship ends. Some are even offered full-time positions with the organization after they graduate; for these students, the community service experience actually serves as a valuable entry into the work world. For others, who may find their experiences in the community placements negative or overwhelming, their sixteen weeks of voluntarism help them define what they do *not* want to do with their lives. This is an important lesson as well.

Reaching Across Boundaries

Feminist community service tests students' abilities to reach across boundaries of difference and to move across the borders that separate theory and practice, classroom and community, and their own conception of themselves as private individuals and public citizens. It also often coincides with their own psychological and emotional movement from late adolescence into adulthood. For some students all of this comes together, and they are able to make these transitions with fluidity and grace; for others, the connections are far more difficult. As one student who took the course wrote, "Studying feminism in the classroom and applying and practicing it in the workplace is not an easy transition."

Through the community service experience, students come to understand differences more deeply. Many of our students at Rutgers self-consciously strove to cross differences of class, race, or age to form bonds with the community women that were based on gender. One thoughtful student wrote, "I know issues of diversity are important to explore within feminism because before we can demand equal rights and treatment based on gender, we must first, or at least simultaneously, establish a community *within* women. An important beginning is including women who have thus far been considered 'other' within the movement. It is therefore important for me to learn about and to be able to relate to, as diverse a group of women as possible."

An important first step in understanding difference is to admit whatever feelings we might have about those we perceive as different. Some of the Rutgers students in the women's studies seminar honestly struggled with their feelings of prejudice and fear toward those with whom they worked in the community who were different from themselves. One such student, for example, volunteered at the New Jersey Women and AIDS Network (NJWAN), an advocacy and education organization for women with HIV or AIDS. A middle-class African American woman and a senior, her struggle with difference, which she spoke about with self-reflection, had to do with the staff with whom she worked at her internship site, rather than with the community they served. She wrote the following in her final paper:

> To the extent that four out of the seven people at NJWAN are lesbians, my work here has forced me to confront my own homophobic attitudes. Here is a journal entry I made after a discussion with my supervisor about her bisexuality: ". . . I just know I feel (and have always felt) uncomfortable around homosexuals, because I don't understand the whole phenomenon. How can two men/women sleep together? It just boggles the mind. Since the internship consists of four lesbians and three straights working in the office, I find it necessary to confront my own homophobic attitudes and deal with them. I'm sure it will be a difficult process, since I hate racists, sexists, and others who can't accept difference. It's hard to realize I may be one of those people."

This student's willingness to confront her own prejudices and make a commitment to "deal with them" is both honest and mature. As Audre Lorde has written, we cannot cross the boundaries that divide us if we do not first recognize our differences. "It is not our differences which separate women," Lorde writes, "but our reluctance to recognize those differences and to deal effectively with the distortions which have resulted from the ignoring and misnaming of those differences" (1992, p. 9). If we recognize those different from us as our equals, she reminds us, we can then use those differences to enrich our visions and strengthen our joint struggles.

The borders that separate theory and practice, classroom and community, can be impassable for some students. One woman we taught who volunteered at a transitional housing development for formerly homeless women fluctuated between identifying with the women residents and firmly separating herself from them. Her job involved counseling the women in parenting, personal growth, health issues, and budgeting skills. The previous semester she had written a research paper on women and poverty; intellectually she understood the complex and interrelated systems of oppression that contribute to poverty and homelessness in America. She wrote: "We have a tendency to look down on homeless people and poor people. We think that they are lazy people who just don't want to work. One thing that I learned while at Amandla Crossing is that anyone can become homeless. Some of these women at Amandla Crossing *were just like us* [emphasis added]. They had beautiful homes, nice cars, and good jobs. A series of events occurred in their lives and they became homeless."

Yet this student, who had immigrated from Jamaica with her family when she was a child and was slightly older than the average student (she was twenty-five), was conflicted and found her experience at the transitional home depressing, stressful, and overwhelming. At times she judged the women at the shelter as people very different from herself, as "other." She wrote:

> This internship was very challenging and overwhelming at times. I was surprised to see how young the women were. The youngest woman at this shelter is sixteen years, and the oldest woman is thirty years. This was really a shock for me. Some of the women are around my age, and many of these women have three or four children. I often look at my life and compare it with the lives of these women. I have accomplished so much. I am about to graduate from Rutgers University with a B.A. Many of these women have not even completed high school. I often wonder how they got to this point.

On the basis of her community service experience at the shelter, this student decided to give up her career goal of becoming a social worker. In fact, she recently requested a recommendation for a job in a bank.

Many students we taught drew on their own life experiences to try to find common ground with the community women. For example, the student described earlier who wrestled with her feelings of homophobia toward the staff of the organization volunteered with a group of women who were HIV-positive or had

AIDS. At first, in class this student (who was shy) had expressed feelings about not having the "right" to speak in front of the women in the group and about being reluctant to present herself as someone who could talk about AIDS in front of this audience, as she herself did not carry the virus or suffer from the disease. "I had not experienced the same oppression as a woman living with AIDS," she remarked. As an African American she knew what it was like to have people speak about her race without knowing anything about her life or her experience, and she did not want to repeat this mistake.

Then, in midsemester this student herself had an illness, which gave her the opportunity to try to understand what it feels like to have AIDS in our society: she caught the measles. Because measles is contagious, she was quarantined for four weeks along with other infected students, and the university launched a major immunization drive for all students, staff, and faculty, and even threatened to shut down if the disease became an epidemic. This student used her own experience of illness—temporary though it was—to give her a bond and a basis for identification with the HIV-infected women. It also gave her a voice and the self-confidence to use it before these women. She wrote the following in her final paper: "After listening to the stories of these women . . . I felt I could identify with them and offer support, based on my bout with the measles and the recollection of how I was treated. It was as if I myself had an incurable virus that someone could 'catch.'" At the end of the semester she described her community service as "a most empowering experience," which "I will carry . . . with me for the rest of my life."

Although her empathy was genuine, this student's need to stress similarities rather than the differences between her experience and that of the women she worked with reveals a complexity posed by community service and raises questions that proponents of service learning must consider thoughtfully. Must differences be obliterated for empathy and understanding to flourish? Is commonality the only basis for connection? Or does a student's attempt to see through another's lens and grasp that person's view, however briefly, provide a starting point for understanding? In emphasizing the value of knowledge gained through experience, do we devalue other means by which we learn? Experiential learning situated within a feminist pedagogy becomes a place to raise these kinds of questions and deepen our conversations about the necessary relationship between experiential and other forms of learning.

Another young woman who used her life experiences differently to reach across difference was a white, middle-class, Jewish student who talked about the commonalities between anti-Semitism and racism with the African American women with whom she volunteered. She wrote:

> I have become involved in some intense discussions about the reasons behind racism between the residents at Amandla Crossing. Once my Judaism came up and that was because the Black woman with whom I was talking said the prejudice she was subjected to was similar to anti-Semitism she had once witnessed. . . . The woman and I agreed that there were similarities between the oppression of Blacks and of Jews in this country. . . . I have been able to relate my own experience as a Jew to a lot of what some of the women have said about being African American.

By having the conversation with women at her placement rather than in her journal or in the classroom this student learned that a perspective she believed in was shared by women whose life experiences were very different.

Students also used the community service experience as an opportunity to consider their own positions in social hierarchies and to recognize their privilege. For these exceptional students, voluntarism offered them a new worldview, one that was accompanied by a commitment to social change and community involvement. A student who volunteered at the American Civil Liberties Union of New Jersey described a "contradiction" she felt every time she went to the Newark office. She described this in her paper:

I had to walk up to the third floor past Superior Cleaning. It is a temporary worker agency with a staff mainly made up of Latina and Black women (the rest are Latino and Black men). I was in stark contrast to them. There I was, a middle-class white student learning, thinking, and working for credits. Not only was I not getting paid, but I was paying to be there. They showed up every morning looking for assignments that break their backs and do not pay well so they can feed themselves and their families. I am still trying to reconcile this situation. I am continually questioning how I am using the privilege I have to work on creating a society without racist and sexist institutions and without such economic disparity.

Noticing and reflecting on the differences between her position as a student and the position of female domestic workers, she is moved to consider how she can act to create a more just and humane society. A student who questions inequality with some experiential knowledge is better educated and more likely to participate as a citizen.

It is clear to us that feminist community service, combined with a course that is academic in content yet allows class time for discussion of the service component, can be a powerful learning experience for students. It can encourage them to reflect critically on their own cultural roots, to explore their own values and emerging commitments, and to develop skills in collaboration and in envisioning situations from multiple perspectives. Community service can help women find their own voices as leaders and advocates, their own position in the history of women's activism.

The Role of Faculty

Faculty members can help students move successfully from the classroom to the community—and by extension from the university to their lives after graduation—by educating them to listen and to cultivate humility and acceptance of difference, and by themselves serving as role models. There are times, even in a democracy, when it is more important to listen than to speak. Students will be best able to forge intercultural partnerships with communities outside of campus by putting aside their own preconceptions and by being willing to listen and learn.

These are important but often overlooked skills to foster in educating democratic citizens and community builders. In *The Call of Service*, child psychiatrist Robert Coles, who is white, says of his research in the 1960s with a six-year-old black girl and her family who led the struggle for school desegregation in Boston: "I don't believe I could have understood Tessie and her family's capacity to live as they did, do as they did for so long, against such great odds, had I not begun to hear what *they* were saying and meaning, what *they* intended others to know about their reasons and values. . . ." (1993, p. 26).

Women's studies faculty in particular have a unique role to play in fostering the development of community service initiatives in the academy. Because their discipline actually grew out of a social movement, their connections to the community should be strong and reciprocal, their commitments to activism and advocacy ongoing. As one feminist theorist wrote, "It is senseless to study the situation of women without a concomitant commitment to do something about it" (Flax, 1993, p. 82). A Rutgers graduate of the course "Community Activism: Women's Participation" reflected similarly on her learning: "I have, through this internship, realized the importance of inclusiveness and activism within feminism. . . . As a Women's Studies student, I think it is important to see the connection between community activism and feminism. You cannot be actively trying to educate and change things for the women of the world without being involved, hands-on, with women, and this internship has given me a good start."

The Challenges of Combining Advocacy and Scholarship

The historical development of women's studies and its continuing marginal position in the university raise important issues for service learning courses, which like women's studies also question existing paradigms and traditional ways of learning. The challenges that women's studies represents to the academy are real; they generate continued perplexity and even suspicion about the status of women's studies as an intellectual rather than a political field. Women's studies' intellectual advocacy of interdisciplinary scholarship, its view of gender as a central analytic category, and its primarily female constituency can cause programs to appear anomalous and even separatist among older, more established, or male-dominated departments. Like other area studies programs founded in the 1960s and 1970s (such as African, Puerto Rican, Hispanic, and Caribbean) whose intellectual roots grew out of political and social movements, women's studies is accused by its critics of confusing affirmative action with scholarship.

Despite the continuing emphasis within women's studies communities on their existence as institutional homes for an intellectual concern about women's issues, programs continue to run into difficulties over where the line between the intellectual and the political lies (Kessler-Harris, 1992). A recent controversy at Rutgers about the women's studies program reveals how complicated the heritage of advocacy and scholarship can become. In this debate the program's goal of building a feminist community with students and other groups, particularly racial and ethnic minorities traditionally underrepresented in governance within university hierarchies, ran up against a different set of assumptions about how to constitute departmental governance. Women's studies practitioners, as part of their effort to put the knowledge and insight gained from scholarship into practice, seek to put their many intellectual and political differences into the conversations that guide their programs. Feminist scholarship has explored the ways in which gender can provide a basis for commonalities among women (DuBois and others, 1987; Harding, 1991; Lorde, 1992). However, as women's history demonstrates, this shared identity as women does not transcend differences among women produced by class, race, ethnicity, sexuality, religion, age, and nationality. Debate among differing perspectives is essential to build programs that are intellectually vital and responsive to their varied constituencies.

The Rutgers program's bylaws seek to foster diversity within the women's studies community by ensuring the presence of underrepresented groups in the governance structure of the program. Goals (some might say quotas) for the representation of ethnic and racial minorities were specified for core women's studies committees. A senior university-wide faculty committee reviewing the program in 1995 perceived these aspirations as evidence that the program was a political rather than an academic enterprise. One possible reading of the committee's conclusions places them within the emerging nationwide debate about affirmative action, opposing the use of numerical targets for creating equality of opportunity for racial and ethnic minorities. This reading is plausible except that the committee made a surprising misreading of the bylaws that revealed its anxiety about women. The committee, none of whom are among the 102 faculty affiliates of the women's studies program, read these provisions as including sexual orientation as a protected category (it isn't). How did this error arise? What does it signify? Possibly a continuing anxiety that women located outside traditional disciplines in the academy are threatening because of their sexuality.

The error the committee made revealed a larger, underlying debate over which criteria are appropriate to use in creating a community and building a curriculum. The committee had no difficulty with provisions that designated participation in the program by faculty rank. Even the presence of students on the committee went unremarked. The efforts of the women's studies program at Rutgers to create a teaching and learning community that reflected its broader democratic, feminist ideals put it into conflict with an alternative definition of community that recognized field, seniority, and status as the appropriate basis for representation. Both definitions are meritorious and each have their own politics, but women's studies' tradition of advocacy makes its politics visible. Women's studies' efforts to give students and racial and ethnic minorities a place at the table still meet with resistance from established constituencies that rely on a different set of criteria for building a collegial community, educating students, and allocating power within the university.

Women's Studies and Service Learning

The location of women's studies on the borders of the traditional disciplines also speaks directly to what women's studies can offer students interested in service learning. Alice Kessler-Harris (1992) has written, "The institutional parallel to the outsider-within perspective, is the outsider status of women's studies within an institution that has its own rules and regulations. The outsider status simultaneously permits us to function with minimal attention to hierarchically and bureaucratically instituted norms and raises questions about how most effectively to relate to power. It thus forces us to negotiate between the competing values of community and hierarchy" (p. 802).

Women's studies is both self-conscious and made aware of its structural and philosophical differences with other disciplines. These differences can produce useful insights about the specificity and limitations of one's experience. Rather than universalizing from limited knowledge, women's studies teaches that in order to go beyond the specific conditions of one's life, one needs a respectful and constant engagement with those differently situated. This is a profound and intellectually challenging position. Students learn that they must go outside the confines of their experience, imaginatively or actually, to learn. They must do this, however, without losing sight of how their own intellectual training and personal experience have shaped them. This kind of reflexivity is particularly useful when students engage in a learning experience that puts citizenship and gender in the foreground.

Women's studies historically has recognized the role education can play in transforming institutions and lives. After all, the insight that the personal is political comes from the women's movement.

Experiential learning can be a catalyst for students to act on insights gained from feminist theory about the ways gender differently constructs men's and women's social, economic, and political situations. Feminist interdisciplinary scholarship can enrich service learning initiatives currently reliant on a literature about democracy and service derived largely from political science.

Service learning and women's studies share an interest in educating students to take an active role in public life, expanding the categories of knowledge and enlarging the community of learners. Despite these mutual interests there have not been extensive discussions between women's studies and service learning teachers. Women's studies focus on gender and diversity and service learning's emphasis on what community means in contemporary American society have the potential to enhance conversations about community, responsibility, citizenship, diversity, rights, and democracy (Barber and Battistoni, 1993). Initiating a dialogue between women's studies practitioners and educators involved in service learning holds the promise of deepening each group's understanding of experiential learning, pedagogy, and citizenship.

Chapter Four

Residential Colleges

Laboratories for Teaching
Through Difference

Grant H. Cornwell, Eve Stoddard

The United States is in the throes of an identity crisis as the emphasis in its motto, *e pluribus unum*, shifts from the one to the many, from the myth of the melting pot to the reality of the patchwork quilt. Institutions of higher education are relatively privileged islands in the larger society that ought to provide experimental spaces for diverse constituencies to find some commonality without shedding their traditions and perspectives. However, despite the media hoopla about the demise of the European American tradition of great books, college campuses mirror the cultural and racial separatism of society at large (Spitzberg and Thorndike, 1992; Sidel, 1994). Colleges should lead the way in developing practices of critical integration, that is, ways in which diverse individuals and groups live and work together through a process of self-reflective scrutiny and criticism. Communities must seek integration in ways that do not sacrifice the self-esteem of women and minority persons. Theoretically, Dewey's *Democracy and Education* ([1916] 1966) points toward ways to implement what we are calling practices of critical integration. And to suggest the real potential and the problems of such an approach, St. Lawrence University's First-Year Program (FYP) has tried since 1987 to bring together first-year students in living-learning communities that actively examine issues of diversity and commonality as the students interact dialectically in academic courses and in social life.

Divisions in the Academy

For the past decade our nation has been debating the problems and promises of cultural pluralism. With regard to higher education this debate has transpired within the unfortunate frame of culture wars, the outrage over Stanford's inclusion of a few non-Western texts in its core curriculum mirroring the dominant society's outrage over affirmative action. Strikingly, within the academy, this protracted conflict has been almost exclusively focused on the content of the curriculum. Alan Bloom's *The Closing of the American Mind* (1987) was paradigmatic in the way it seized the rhetoric of open-mindedness for the side of the traditionalists. Dinesh D'Souza (1991) and others followed this up by claiming academic rigor for the traditionalist side as well. Those who have written on behalf of a more inclusive curriculum, such as Henry Louis Gates Jr. (1992), bell hooks (1994), Cornel West (1993b), and Gloria Anzaldua (1987), have received less attention outside the academy. While the academic curriculum is undoubtedly worth fighting about, because it signifies what history is and which cultural contributions count, the exclusivity of the attention paid to it betrays a prejudice shared by all concerned, a prejudice of those whose lives have been formed by and are now devoted to letters.

Surely books matter a great deal; to some extent colleges are culturally constructed havens set aside for students to be influenced by what they read. But given that liberal education is the training ground for many of society's leaders in politics, industry, education, and the professions, and that academia might lead the way in thinking about the dilemmas of cultural diversity facing the United States today, the curricular debates completely fail to consider the lived context in which student reading takes place. What is missing is an adequate consideration of the fact that reading takes place on college campuses, and that these campuses are sites where

American cultural pluralism is experienced daily and directly in ways that students have not before encountered as intimately. As Ruth Sidel (1994) writes:

> Higher education in the United States today mirrors, just as it did in earlier eras, the values, the divisions, and the debates within the larger society. . . . Because many institutions of higher learning are enclosed, somewhat isolated communities in which different kinds of people spend an unusual amount of time together, highly charged issues and incidents are quickly magnified and erupt into full-blown conflict. Many colleges, in fact, resemble "total institutions," as described by Erving Goffman, in which the participants eat, sleep, work, and play in the same environment, and feelings and actions can quickly escalate until they are very nearly out of control [p. 8].

Books are read and talked about by students in residence halls, in libraries, in dining halls. For most students college life falls into two sharply differentiated arenas: the classroom and social life. Unfortunately, students often do not see any connections between the content of the curriculum and the lives they are negotiating as residents of a college campus. This is evidence of the extent to which higher education continues rather than challenges the alienation students come to expect in schooling. In all cases this alienation signals a deep kind of failure, but with respect to educating students to live and work in our culturally diverse democracy, the failure is especially critical.

Thus, one of our main purposes in this chapter is to argue that the organization of higher education mitigates against a vital dialectic between academic inquiry and lived experience, whether that dialectic exists within the individual college student or between academia and the larger world of U.S. society. Institutional structures, and the cultures they create, could not be more powerfully designed to keep student experience and intellectual inquiry apart. Without any sense of irony or disappointment, the work of colleges is organized into divisions: academic affairs has purview over what goes on inside the classroom, student affairs over what goes on outside. One result is that the persons working within these divisions have attitudes toward one another that are frequently marked by distrust and disparagement. Faculty on many campuses have little regard for student affairs professionals, and they construct elaborate principles that justify their noninvolvement in the lives of students outside their classrooms. They say, "I don't want to know about students' lives because I don't want to be biased in judging their academic work," or "I am trained in my discipline, not in counseling or community organizing."

On the other side, student affairs professionals, from counselors to residential life staff, consider it their primary mission to create a climate that is safe and therapeutic, where students can escape from the pressures of studying. Faculty are portrayed as insensitive to the needs of "the whole student." The result of these divisions is that students are implicitly and explicitly told that the two domains of college life have nothing to do with one another.

Dewey and Democratic Education

We are interested in exploring the extent to which college campuses could or should be laboratories for democratic pluralism. Can the process of living together educate students for participation in a culturally diverse democracy? The experience at St. Lawrence suggests that the answer is a cautious, skeptical yes. We have found the educational theory of John Dewey a useful approach to experimenting with diversity across the academic-social divide. In *Democracy and Education* ([1916] 1966), Dewey talks about education as the critical reorganization and reconstruction of experience, whereby meaning is increased by perceiving continuities and connections between thought and action. As Dewey writes, "The very process of living together educates; it enlarges and enlightens experience; it stimulates and enriches imagination; it creates responsibility" (p. 6). If the diversity students wrestle with in their day-to-day lives were brought under the kind of critical scrutiny we customarily bring to texts, if their experiences were worked with, worked over, talked about, and analyzed, it would occasion genuine learning. Dewey laments the separation of academic inquiry and student experience: "Save by accident, out-of-school experience is left in its crude and comparatively irreflective state. It is not subject to the refining and expanding influences of the more accurate and comprehensive material of direct instruction. The latter is not motivated and impregnated with a sense of reality by being inter-mingled with the realities of everyday life. The best type of teaching bears in mind the desirability of effecting this interconnection. It puts the student in the habitual attitude of finding points of contact and mutual bearings" (p. 163).

According to Dewey, democratic education operates through praxis; ideas are "anticipations of possible solutions" and are tested by acting on them ([1916] 1966, p. 160). Dewey accuses faculty of supplying ready-made ideas by the thousands but then failing to attend to their being experimented with, engaged, or employed in experience. Thus we may have more culturally diverse campuses and more multicultural curricula, but if they are not subjected to critical scrutiny across the borders of classroom and residence, the de facto segregation of the larger society will continue.

For Dewey the fundamental aim of education is to prepare students to participate in democratic society; however, democracy is understood not as a form of government but as a "mode of associated living, of conjoint communicated experience" (p. 87). Dewey asserts, "There is more than a verbal tie between the words common, community, and communication. Men live in a community in virtue of the things which they have in common; and communication is the way in which they come to possess things in common" (p. 4).

Thus communication is logically prior to community; it is the vehicle that might carry diverse persons toward community. In fact, communities can be evaluated according to the quality of communication possible within them. Dewey would have us ask, "How numerous and varied are the interests which are consciously shared? How full and free is the interplay with other forms of association?" ([1916] 1966, p. 83). In democratic communities, "[t]here are many interests consciously communicated and shared; and there are varied and free points of contact with other modes of association" (p. 83). Insofar as communication is inhibited, not free, not open, not varied, the kind of community Dewey posits as desirable is precluded. College campuses have long been thought of as bastions of free speech, as spaces in the larger society where it should be safe to experiment with and express all kinds of ideas. Thus college campuses *should* be ideal locations for the development of democratic communities. But a question remains about how diversity affects the possibility of the kind of communication Dewey sees as essential to democracy. That is, how do the socially constructed differences of race, ethnicity, class, gender, age, and sexual orientation affect the quality of communication that is possible among our students on our campuses? Although we might criticize Dewey for his overreaching optimism, he is not unaware of how inequality disrupts communication. Dewey says that with inequalities of power and privilege,

> there is no extensive number of common interests; there is no free
> play back and forth among the members of a social group. . . . In
> order to have a large number of values in common, all members of
> the group must have an equable opportunity to receive and to take
> from others. There must be a large variety of shared undertakings
> and experiences. Otherwise the experiences which educate some
> into masters, educate others into slaves. And the experience of each
> party loses meaning, when the free interchange of varying modes of
> life-experience is arrested [(1916) 1966, p. 84].

Separation into identity groups that do not communicate prevents a dynamic that Dewey calls "social endosmosis" (p. 84). The boundaries of vital democratic communities are like permeable membranes, and it is crucial that the ideas and experiences of marginal groups enter and challenge the discourse of the majority. Without this kind of permeability, all suffer.

Thus Dewey would see pluralism as both epistemologically and politically important. Epistemologically, "diversity of stimulation means novelty, and novelty means challenge to thought" (p. 85). Dewey continues: "These more numerous and more varied points of contact denote a greater diversity of stimuli to which an individual has to respond; they consequently put a premium on variation in his action. They secure a liberation of powers which remain suppressed as long as the incitations to action are partial, as they must be in a group which in its exclusiveness shuts out many interests" (p. 87).

Notice the type of critique Dewey would level against the kinds of separatism found on college campuses. The loss of educative potential affects the bases of how learning takes place. Arguing against separatism for its corrosive effects on communication, Dewey writes: "The isolation and exclusiveness of a gang or clique brings its antisocial spirit into relief. But this same spirit is found wherever one group has interests 'of its own' which shut it out from full interaction with other groups, so that its prevailing purpose is the protection of what it has got, instead of reorganization and progress through wider relationships" (p. 86).

Thus Dewey would oppose as inimical to the point and process of education any kind of social group that seeks homogeneity and separate identity, including not only exclusive fraternities and sororities but separatist black student unions, women's theme houses, and the like. When groups isolate they do not communicate. When they do not communicate, their members are not stimulated by having to engage diversity, and growth and learning are thereby stifled.

In addition to discussing its cognitive role, Dewey affirms the importance of pluralism in fulfilling the social role of education; without communication, the experimental social construction of democratic communities is precluded. Thus Dewey sees great promise in engaging diversity: "The extension in space of the number of individuals who participate in an interest so that each has to refer his own action to that of others, and to consider the action of others to give point and direction to his own, is equivalent to the breaking down of those barriers of class, race, and national territory which kept men from perceiving the full import of their activity" (p. 87).

Dewey maintains that open communication of experience among diverse individuals breaks down "the barriers of social stratification which make individuals impervious to the interests of others" (p. 120). Intelligent sympathy, Dewey says, is more than a feeling: "it is a cultivated imagination for what men have in common and a rebellion at what unnecessarily divides them" (p. 121). All Dewey's hopes for the achievement of democratic communities, in and through educative processes, rest on "communication." This optimistic faith in the possibility and efficacy of communication in establishing a public discourse that can overcome differences can be traced directly to the Enlightenment. The town meetings that still govern many New England towns are a continuing testament to this faith, which was grounded in a universalist paradigm of human nature.

Problemizing Communication

The dominant premises of Enlightenment thinkers were that all individuals share a common capacity for reason and morality, and that all cultural differences are relatively superficial effects of socialization. Different practices and beliefs can be stripped away to show the common humanity beneath them. Also, because cultural differences are constructed through education, changing education and socialization processes can change society. By cutting across the opposition between reason and experience, Dewey's pragmatic methodology marks an advance over Enlightenment philosophies of social and political change. However, in his appeal to "communication," Dewey remains stuck in the Enlightenment's view of a universal human nature, a representational language, and a unitary individual self. He writes as if persons associated together for a common purpose, such as running a town or joining a university, could simply use language as a transparent medium for exchanging viewpoints and ideas, with no hint of the multifarious impediments posed by questions about the referentiality of language and about the multiple and unequal subject-positions of the speakers, particularly in a "multicultural" group of people.

Before considering the question of language itself, we might note that the difficulties in intercultural and even intergender communication seem much deeper than Dewey believes. We would guess that this is because his models of community and communication assume that the codes of the dominant culture, class, and gender will govern communication; those for whom these codes are alien will learn to use them. However, even where assimilation to a dominant discourse is the goal, cultural differences can be insurmountable or, more dangerous, unrecognized. Thus in a classroom, students from a culture that values passivity and silence will be regarded as failing to participate or unprepared or uninterested. Students from a background that values obedience to authority will be disadvantaged in a course on critical thinking. Students who grew up in an arena where physical fighting was a normal way of working out conflicts will be thrown out of college before they have a chance to participate. These are some of the more glaring issues that must be addressed before we can turn to "communication" as the basis for democratic education. But theoretical analyses of language and subjectivity complicate the issue further.

During the past thirty years, there has been an explosion of scholarship on the problematics of language, much of it originating with Russian formalism and structuralist linguistics (Bann, 1973; Derrida, 1976, 1978; Foucault, 1977; Saussure, 1959). The complex relations between language and the construction of subjectivity have been posited by structuralism and poststructuralism, feminists on both sides of the Atlantic, and postcolonialists from Gayatri Spivak (1987) to Ngugi wa Thiong'o (1972).

We could not possibly do justice to the Enlightenment critiques inscribed in these huge areas of theory, but we want to suggest that they cast doubt on the sufficiency of Dewey's appeal to "communication" for balancing difference and commonality on American college campuses, let alone in the larger polities that constitute the United States. Much of this theory is about the ways in which language powerfully structures subjectivity and experience, while at the same time failing to operate referentially. Discourse thus simultaneously structures power and knowledge and remains itself ungovernable, always carrying layers of encrusted and unintended meanings, both overdetermining the speaker's meaning and obscuring it (Derrida, 1976, 1978; Foucault, 1977, 1980).

Dewey ([1916] 1966) professes to value the richness and complexity that diversity brings to a community and to believe that associated living can bring persons together without obliterating their differences. However, he definitely values assimilation over a diversity that would enforce separation. His optimism indicates a naiveté about the deep epistemological, ethical, and power differentials that structure the relationships of various individuals to specific communicative situations. Franz Fanon's description ([1963] 1968) of colonized subjectivities marked the beginning of a long line of fictional and analytical accounts of the ways colonialism fractures the identities of the colonized. In any situation (including that of the United States today) where there is one language that belongs to the powerful, to the law, the government, the educational system, and perhaps to men, and other languages or dialects that structure the home lives of the disempowered, the choice of dialect or language becomes a power issue. The same dilemmas operate in the privileging of Standard English on an American college campus as in the Kenyan government or an international forum on AIDS. The members of the group have to use English because it is the most widely used language and therefore practical to use. But English is widely known because of the earlier predominance of the British Empire, followed by America's ascendency to the dominant world military and economic power. Encoded in the triumph of English are all kinds of judgments about ethnic and cultural superiority that then infuse the subjectivity of the colonized speaker so as to challenge her relationship to the language and to her native language and culture.

When a group of students forms a campus community in the United States, unless they are an exclusively ethnic group they will in most cases use a dialect of English close to Standard American English. They will behave with etiquette established by middle-class European American culture. Unless they are all women, masculine codes of behavior and interaction will probably govern the discussion. Individuals who would be more comfortable with a different language or a different style of communication must conform, if they are able to, or not participate. Postcolonial studies and women's studies tell us that in many cases people do conform or assimilate, but they are left with feelings of low self-esteem or even self-hatred. If they cannot conform or they resist, they cannot participate and are left outside the structures of power. Many children of color never make it to high school graduation because the community established by the public school system does not speak to them. Many girls drop out of math because its discourse community excludes them.

From an Enlightenment perspective, educating colonized subjects into the language and culture of the powerful is a step toward achieving universal peace. It is certainly a means for individuals to gain access to the goods of material success. But its cost is a divided subjectivity that internalizes unequal power relations and the dominant culture's denigration of the subjugated one. The individual's own mind, constructed through competing and unequally valued discourses, becomes caught in a conflict between upward mobility and material success on the one hand, and a lived experience that connects with early childhood enculturation, family, and organic community on the other.

Although we recognize the ways that academic theories about language, power, and subjectivity challenge Dewey's optimistic trust in human communication for building democratic communities, we nonetheless believe that diverse communities are necessary.

And Dewey's theories point us toward praxis as the method for transcending the difficulties posed by the unequal and segregationist society in which we find ourselves. Before moving on to an examination of St. Lawrence's experiment in Deweyan education, we will put it in context by providing a look at the realities of "diversity" on American college campuses and at the relative merits of separatist as opposed to integrated campus communities.

Diversity on Campus

In their recent study for the Carnegie Foundation, Irving J. Spitzberg, Jr., and Virginia V. Thorndike (1992) found that in a range of colleges and universities across the United States, "[r]acial and ethnic differences as well as gender differences often significantly shape the climate on our campuses, both explicitly and implicitly" (p. 28). They conclude that "[d]ifferential treatment of all undergraduates on the basis of sex as well as race and ethnicity is common on the nation's campuses, both in and out of the classroom" (p. 64). Women have had increasing access to higher education throughout the twentieth century, but only over the past twenty years have U.S. campuses seen increasing numbers of nonwhite, non–European American students. Nonetheless, "[t]he overwhelming majority of all students come to college having had little contact with other races and ethnicities before attending college; even fewer have had any education about differences" (p. 35).

The word *diversity* encompasses all kinds of differences—racial, class, and gender to name a few—but it retains the white, middle-class, heterosexual male as the norm. A "diversity" requirement might be fulfilled by a course in African American literature or gay studies but not by a course on nineteenth-century American literature. This is a conceptual problem we have to confront when trying to discuss diversity, whether of students or segments of society or the curriculum. Who or what is diverse, and why? In focusing on campus life, on how students belong to the campus community, the main categories are usually race, ethnicity, gender, sexual preference, and, to a lesser degree, age and ability. In ordinary discourse, if a student is "diverse," he or she "has" one of these traits: race = nonwhite, gender = nonmale, sexual preference = nonheterosexual, age = nontraditional or older.

This particular take on diversity marginalizes other groups who also do not fit with the "norm" of white, middle-class, heterosexual male. At St. Lawrence, for example, white students from the local area known as the North Country, a group of six rural, poor counties several hours distant from any city, often feel and appear very different from the dominant groups of students who come from the New York and Boston metropolitan areas. The North Country students also fall into two groups related to academic strengths. The majority are courted as extremely talented scholarship students selected by local high schools, but some of the less advantaged come through the Higher Education Opportunity Program (HEOP). The latter then are further differentiated from the nonwhite majority of HEOP students who are recruited from inner-city schools in the Bronx and Buffalo. Students of color are differentiated by class and academic skills into regular admits and HEOP students. Some African American students come from affluent prep school backgrounds where they have been in a largely white environment; others come from largely segregated inner-city neighborhoods and high schools. Some students come from West Indian heritages, and some have roots in the rural South. Some are Latina or Latino, and many are not. These are but a few examples of the kinds of complex diversity one can identify through race and class. A key point is that although some kinds of diversity are visible to any observer, many are not. Well-intentioned efforts to support diversity can end up squelching it by organizing the social world into a few crude categories: white and black, male and female, rich and poor. Any college campus has to work organically with its local conditions. At a women's college, a white male is diverse, as he would be at a historically black college.

Although women are not a minority in society or on campuses, their historically lower status and restriction to the private domain has resulted in unequal representation in the subject matter of higher education and in unequal treatment in both social and academic spheres. Thus even white, middle-class women experience marginalization and victimization on college campuses. But their experiences are not necessarily parallel to those of other marginalized groups, and women's values and attitudes are deeply affected by their other identities, especially race or ethnicity but also class. And as Spitzberg and Thorndike (1992) point out, "Unlike minorities, however, who have a social and often political context in which to situate discriminatory behavior, most undergraduate women do not" (p. 64). "Unconscious attitudes, poor taste, insensitivity and ingrained stereotypes are the most pervasive form of sexism undergraduate women encounter" (p. 59). Their "visits confirm that, for the most part, men are still the educational norm against which women are evaluated. The curriculum has remained substantially unchanged" (p. 63). Since the "waning of feminist consciousness in the 1980s" (p. 60), most campus attention related to gender is focused on violence against women and not on issues related to learning, achievement, or leadership. Women of color often feel forced to choose between allegiance to their ethnic group and identification with women's issues, and most often the latter is sacrificed to the former. Because African American males in our society are so embattled, African American women in particular often feel that they must put support for their race before their own welfare as women.

If we look at campus life with regard to the practice and discourse of cultural pluralism, what we find is that all of the inertia is toward separatism. Dining halls, social spaces, study spaces, and in many cases residences are marked by cultural separatism. Many campus organizations are, by definition, identity groups that seek, implicitly or explicitly, to provide association for students culturally similar to one another. Fraternities and sororities are, by their charters, separatist with regard to gender, but they are also notorious for being separatist with regard to class and ethnicity. Finally, and most pointedly, nearly all college campuses have housing options whereby students can choose to self-segregate.

Ironically, the dominant culture within and outside of college campuses views separatism and identity politics as the choice of minority groups. White students often comment on their perceived difficulty in mixing with students of color, whom they regard as isolationist and rejecting. However, the reverse is in fact true: white students isolate themselves from contact with students of color, whereas students of color mix frequently with white students. No one looks at an all-white residence hall or classroom and labels it "separatist." It is regarded as the norm. If there were no students of color majoring in English on a particular campus, people would not be likely to label the English department separatist or accuse it of practicing identity politics. Yet when a theme cottage devoted to black culture is inhabited by only black students or when an African American Studies minor is filled with African American students, it is labeled separatist. But blame is not the key issue here. The point is that we still by and large have a racially segregated society, both on and off campus. There is obviously a big difference between legally mandated apartheid and self-segregation of minority groups for solidarity, but ultimately societies need to find some common ground.

Of course, there is mounting evidence that certain forms of institutionalized separatism are beneficial to certain marginalized or disempowered groups. Frank Matthews, publisher of *Black Issues in Higher Education,* states: "African-Americans do better at historically black colleges and universities, Asian-Americans at Berkeley, Hispanics at the University of Texas at Austin and in Puerto Rico, and Native Americans increasingly at Southeastern Oklahoma State University. Instead of us moving closer and closer to integration, we seem to be moving closer to racial polarization" (Sidel, 1994, p. 45). An MIT survey of African American alumni found the following: "Three-quarters of those who lived in predominantly white living-group settings described their experiences there in generally negative or mixed terms, while those who lived in predominantly black living-group settings (approximately one-third of the respondents) were unanimously positive about their experience there" (Spitzberg and Thorndike, 1992, p. 35).

The received wisdom in minority affairs offices of college campuses has been that students of color on predominantly white campuses need the support system provided by identity group residences. Many students of color feel that they are already making a huge effort at integration by attending a largely white campus, where they spend most of their time in predominantly white classes, organizations, and offices. Thus in the larger picture of their entire day, the time they spend eating and sleeping with a group of "similar" students is limited. Most white students, on the other hand, spend their entire twenty-four hours among exclusively white students. This suggests that the burden is on the majority to develop greater interaction with those perceived to be different. Educational institutions need to do more to promote reflection by white students on their responsibility to acquaint themselves with students from diverse backgrounds and ethnic groups. As it is now, students of color on predominantly white campuses are still suffering the effects of racism. For example, there is evidence that "movement of African-American males into Ph.D. programs which would train them to be college professors and hence role models for future generations of African-American students is impeded by overt and implicit prejudice" (Sidel, 1994, p. 46).

If white, middle-class males represent the norm around which universities have developed curricula and institutional cultures, then women, working-class students, and students of color occupy marginal positions. Like African Americans, women have often been erased from the histories that structure the curriculum of the humanities; like students of color, women students are often subtly steered away from subjects thought too challenging for them. Yet unlike persons of color, women represent a majority in society and on most campuses, and white women sometimes partake of the privileges of whiteness and middle-class status, and they mingle intimately with white men. Thus most women, unless they choose to attend all-female schools, cannot separate from men in the same way that persons of color can separate from whites. Small groups of radical feminists often do live separately, as do sorority women on college campuses. But the majority of women live in coed situations.

Nonetheless, there is considerable evidence that women benefit from separation. On the basis of "common sense," most people believe that in order to prepare for life in the work world, women would do better to be educated alongside men. Yet studies show that women who attend women's colleges have greater educational and career achievements than those who attend coeducational institutions. For example, except in the case of women at women's colleges, women's self-esteem decreases during their four years of college, while men's self-esteem increases. This decrease in female self-esteem is part of a process that begins at puberty and is thought to play a role in girls' decreases in math performance during the high school years. Furthermore, a "significant amount of data suggest that graduates of women's colleges are overrepresented with respect to graduate degrees awarded and the number of academic distinctions obtained" (Monaco and Gaier, 1992, p. 581). Considering that the academic content has not traditionally been different at women's colleges, the differing levels of achievement must be due to other elements of the campus climate. Some studies suggest that females rely more heavily on role models and on recognition than do males. And in coed settings, women "traditionally neither hold the highest offices nor obtain a proportionate share of financial aid or scholarships" (Monaco and Gaier, p. 580). Single-sex settings make clear the importance of education for women and ensure that women will have access to leadership roles and academic recognition.

Bernice Sandler's work on the "chilly climate" on campus for women (1984) outlines many ways in which women receive messages that their nature is to be feminine and attractive rather than intellectual and achievement-oriented. Sandler writes: "Even those most concerned about equity may inadvertently treat women in ways that convey a powerful subtle or not so subtle message to women—and to men—that somehow women are not as serious professionally, or as capable as their male peers, nor are they expected to be forceful leaders, to achieve at the same level or to participate in formal and informal activities as fully, as actively, or as successfully" (p. 2). Women still are underrepresented in such fields as science and engineering, and they still receive subtle messages that these are masculine fields.

All-female institutions remove socially constructed conflicts between feminine role expectations and behaviors that lead to high achievement, such as independence and assertiveness. If femininity, as Susan Brownmiller (1984) suggests, consists essentially of subordination to men, it becomes irrelevant in an all-female setting. In a group where everyone is a woman, the emphasis will shift to other aspects of identity, such as individual talents and skills.

Dilemmas of Separatism

We are led to conclude that integration can cause serious harm to the self-confidence, personal development, and academic success of some students. But what does this say about the possibility of creating a pluralist democracy? If campus life (whether self-consciously or not) is practice for civic life, then what are colleges preparing students for? Both the positive outcomes of institutionalized separatism and the negative outcomes of compulsory integration suggest only how deep and compelling the problems of cultural pluralism are. Institutionalized separatism is a form of acquiescence, of surrender, of giving up. Separatism as a strategy for empowerment acknowledges that the distribution of power in our culture is indeed attached to gender and ethnicity. The problem with this strategy is that it reproduces, even reifies, the status quo, postponing to some postgraduate setting—the workplace, the neighborhood—the work that needs to be done in learning to live with diversity. Institutionalized separatism is thus an abdication of responsibility on the part of colleges, because no cultural site is as well equipped to do this work as the college campus. At the same time, all experience suggests that merely throwing students together on the basis of some high principle of integration and equality can be harmful to all concerned, and counterproductive to the goals of education for democracy, if not done with great care.

The separatist inertia on college campuses, as in American culture, needs to be an overt topic for critical reflection. An examination of issues of American cultural pluralism in the classroom is
bankrupt without applying it directly to how students choose to
live. We would do well to treat the campus as a laboratory for
democratic pluralism by making it the subject of scrutiny in the
classroom and out. While college campuses mirror the multiplicity
of our culture, by their charter and structure colleges are set up to
work with the tensions and to elicit the potentials of cultural diversity. To do this responsibly, however, will call for a kind of collaboration that is possible only if certain traditional divisions of labor
in the academy are systematically undone. If we are going to practice pluralism we need curricular and co-curricular structures that
involve faculty and staff in every dimension of this very difficult,
very important experiment. The divisions between the classroom
and the campus—divisions that are structurally entrenched in the
organization of traditional college administrations—have to be
transgressed.

St. Lawrence's First-Year Program

The First-Year Program (FYP) at St. Lawrence University has wrestled with these issues since its inception in 1987. Although the program was not initially designed to focus on social and cultural
diversity within a campus community, as soon as faculty became
involved in residential life they were faced with diversity issues,
particularly those of gender, lifestyle, and class.

Faculty created the program as a response to several local and
particular concerns about teaching and learning, concerns that
proved to be prophetic of national critiques of higher education.
First, faculty were concerned that students were not being given a
sufficient orientation to liberal learning. The architecture of the
curriculum, in which knowledge had been broken into highly specific fields, disciplines, and departments, was too fragmented for students to find their way through it in coherent ways.

Second, students were coming to St. Lawrence with communication skills insufficient for college-level work. Composition 101 was not adequately addressing the needs of students with regard to proficient writing and speaking.

Third, the advising relationships between students and faculty were awkward, shallow, and bureaucratic. The traditional first-year advising system, in which adviser and student typically had little basis for a relationship, did not encourage the quality of student-faculty relations essential to liberal education.

Finally, faculty were frustrated with the extent to which the academic and social dimensions of college life were bifurcated. Students were living dual lives: what happened in the classroom seemed to have little bearing on campus life, and vice versa. And at the time, the mid-eighties, campus culture was permeated by a conservative and apathetic contentment with the status quo, which was dominated by upper-middle-class white males.

These concerns gave rise to the design of the FYP. The FYP has four components, each of which can be mapped to one of the original concerns that gave birth to the program, though the overarching goal is the integration of the parts into a comprehensive educational experience for students and faculty alike.

The most radical and ambitious component of the FYP is its living-learning design. In groups of fifty, all first-year students live in residences organized around a required course. Called residential colleges, these living-learning units are staffed by a team that cuts across major structural divisions of the university: students, faculty, and residential life professionals. Each team consists of the following: three faculty members who team teach the course and serve as academic advisers to the students; two or three upper-division students who serve as college assistants (CAs); one upper-division student mentor, or tutor; and a professional residential coordinator (RC).

The intention of this design is to affect the quality of student culture at St. Lawrence through the integration of academic and social experience. The ideal is that FYP colleges develop into communities of learners who value intellectual collaboration and critical reflection. Conversations begun in the classroom are continued in the residence halls; theories, ideas, beliefs, and values are examined, evaluated, measured against students' experience, and picked up again when class reconvenes. In these colleges collaboration and cooperation on readings, papers, and projects help students discover one another as co-learners, as different persons with different strengths and interests who have come to St. Lawrence to engage in a common project. Thus, the goal of living and learning together is to help students understand how critical intellectual inquiry can directly inform their experience, both subjectively—in their individual reflection on their identity, beliefs, and values— and socially, in the choices they make in how they live together.

The second component is an integrated advising system. First-year colleges meet twice a week for team-taught lectures and twice a week in seminars. Students' seminar instructors are also their academic advisers. What this means is that FYP faculty advise students whom they see four times a week, in classes large and small. The quality and quantity of contact between faculty and students in the FYP make possible the kind of close, personal relationships necessary for the giving and receiving of meaningful advice. Faculty can help students chart their academic plans knowing the students' strengths and weaknesses, their hopes and interests.

The intention was to make possible a relation wherein the role of the adviser is not simply to inform the students of their academic requirements but to work with them to envision and project academic plans particular to each individual student. However, the breaking down of barriers between social and academic arenas means that faculty advisers know their advisees as whole persons; they know when students have disciplinary problems and emotional problems; they go on field trips with them and occasionally enter their dorm rooms. This puts faculty in a position to draw on students' experiences for advising and teaching in entirely new ways.

The academic curriculum comprises the third and fourth components of the FYP: course content and communication skills. The communication skills component was designed in response to the mounting research done on composition and critical thinking. These skills, traditionally addressed explicitly only in courses devoted to them, are best developed across the curriculum as part of the teaching and learning in every course. Reading, writing, speaking, and research are complex intellectual and social activities that are at the heart of liberal education; improving students' abilities in these activities requires sustained practice and overt, in-class reflection on that practice. The goals of the communication skills component of the FYP are (1) to help students become more effective writers and speakers, better able to express themselves clearly and gracefully in a variety of forms and in a variety of rhetorical situations; (2) to increase students' fluency and verbal self-confidence; (3) to make students more critical consumers of written, oral, and visual texts; (4) to increase students' awareness and appreciation of writing and speaking as ways of learning, as well as ways of communicating; and (5) to increase students' ability to conduct a research project from start to finish. What we have discovered in the course of this work is that communication skills, the drawing out of student voices, are critical to the development of the FYP colleges and communities.

The fourth component is a two-semester, team-taught, multi-disciplinary course that examines certain general, enduring, and fundamental human questions. Every first-year student at St. Lawrence is enrolled in one of these courses. The organizing themes of the courses, developed by the faculty teams who teach them, are chosen so as to intersect with many issues related to what students experience as they try to negotiate relationships between individuality and community in the residence hall.

Diversity and Community in the FYP

Although the original impetus for the FYP did not include educating students for democracy, as soon as the pilot faculty began to work on implementing and then teaching the program, the centrality of social organization, community and difference, and rights and obligations jumped to the forefront. We knew that we wanted to traverse the boundaries between academic and social life, to bring them to bear on each other dialectically, and once we began to do it, we entered a morass of differences. Faculty learned about acquaintance rape, alcohol poisoning, racial epithets, homophobic graffiti, and general tactics of silencing those on the margins—in ways they never dreamed of sitting in their library carrels in graduate school.

What the faculty and residential staff did not anticipate, but discovered poignantly in the pilot year, was that learning to understand, negotiate, and live with differences was at the center of students' lives in the program, and that the structure of the program brought issues of diversity to the fore. The program presented these issues in their depth, complexity, and in some cases intractability. Looking back, we see the early aspirations of the program as idealistic and naive. Faculty thought that examining issues of diversity in the classroom would bring students to critical consciousness of these issues in student culture, and would even empower some to challenge traditional hierarchies. Student development professionals thought that workshops on diversity, self-governance, and conflict mediation would equip students to negotiate their lives together, and that these residential colleges could become working models of participatory, democratic pluralism.

Gender Conflict in an FYP College

To illustrate the kinds of conflicts and tensions that emerge when the social lives of student communities are taken as seriously as students' academic progress, we will narrate the gender conflicts in one first-year college in the initial stages of the FYP.

It was the 1988–89 academic year, and like many similar institutions, St. Lawrence had not acknowledged that acquaintance rape or sexual harassment were pressing issues on campus. Faculty generally accepted the view that students should be left alone to conduct their private lives, and the student affairs staff took a therapeutic approach to any major problems or infractions of rules.

In one FYP college, an acquaintance rape occurred between two students during the second weekend of the semester, though it did not come to the faculty's attention for about five weeks. Groups of students in the dorm knew one side of it or the other, and trouble fermented quietly. But as it fermented, it bubbled up into relations between the college assistants (CAs) and the residents and among the faculty, two of whom were women. The male involved in the rape lived on the second floor, where there happened accidentally to be a majority of male students. The male freshmen had bonded rapidly and got along extremely well with their CA. The female CA was somewhat timid and did not provide support for the female students equivalent to that provided for the males on the second floor by the male CA.

Symptoms of the polarization occurring among the students began to appear but were indecipherable at first. One of the things the FYP has taught us is how conflicts over difference play themselves out indirectly, through conflicts about noise or through seating and participation patterns in the classroom. In this case, they manifested themselves as hostility toward feminism, in both the classroom and the dorm. The first instance involved the election of officers for the college's community council in the third week of the term. Two very articulate and outspoken women who had emerged as leaders from the time of orientation wanted to run as co-presidents, and at first everyone seemed happy with that. But at the meeting held to organize the community, there appeared a new candidate for president, a male athlete who was well liked but not very talkative or much of a presence heretofore. He won by about a two-thirds majority, and the scuttlebutt was that he was pushed in by the second-floor students, who explicitly did not want the two women running the college. The two women were now labeled as feminists by this group of students. It later turned out that one of these women was the roommate of the woman who had been raped and that she had been openly critical of the male student involved.

Thus, although we did not know it at the time, the election actually was a response to the rape and its aftermath. Under ordinary
teaching circumstances, faculty would never have found out about
this incident, and in all likelihood the woman student would have
dropped out of school. Additionally, destructive patterns of gender
relations would have been reinforced as part of the hegemonic student culture.

As part of the common course at that time the program was
committed to teaching about feminism and to using texts representing women's writing and views. In the introductory "Ways of
Knowing" module of the course, the class read and discussed *Trifles*,
a play that contrasts women's and men's ways of reading domestic
signs at the site of a murder. In the seminar following the lecture-
discussion of the play, the woman professor who taught it had her
seminar students do a freewrite on their response to the day's class,
because she had sensed hostility. More than half the seminar students, predominantly men but also women, found the idea of
women's ways of knowing, especially knowing better than men,
offensive. This kind of informal writing and evaluation plays an
important role in building a common discourse and open communication in the FYP. One very large football player wrote and
repeated orally that he was fed up with feminism and that if the
professor ever brought it up again, he would storm out of class.
Because she was able to elicit this direct response from her seminar
students, this instructor was able to confront directly the students'
beliefs that feminism was equivalent to man-hating, and to build a
basis for trust with those fifteen students.

Eventually the woman who had been raped became so dis-
tressed that she confided in the two female faculty members, who
then sought redress from the campus authorities. Naively assuming
that they would get help from the experts in student affairs, they
found that there was no process for dealing with sexual assault and
that it could be handled only by counseling for the two students
involved. This proved to be the beginning of a major campus initiative to confront issues of sexual ethics and to set up disciplinary

processes for cases of sexual assault. Yet the campus policies took a year to develop and could not provide relief to the woman involved in this case. Increasingly, she felt ostracized in the dorm, where the majority of the support went to the male involved. The women faculty wanted the male student moved out of the college, but no one would allow it. Thus faculty involvement in the residence led to experiences that resulted in major political changes for the whole campus. The woman who had been raped was severely damaged, but by participating in the teach-in and being part of the general ferment that led to creation of the Women's Resource Center, she was empowered to move from victimization to critical reflection and agency.

Over the rest of the year, the power dynamics and gender attitudes within the college changed. The faculty and one sympathetic student development staff person held workshops on sexual assault and discussed them in light of readings being done in class about the relationship between the individual and the community. Most important was the constant effort to build a sense of community trust and thereby communicate about and in spite of differences. This was effected in part through the use of collaborative written and oral projects that brought the students together outside and inside the classroom to do research, to script roles, and to create performances. As they overcame their hostilities in order to perform together, they learned to separate "difference" from hostility. With fairly constant prompting from the faculty, the students developed the ability to discuss women's issues and feminism less defensively and to respect them as legitimate even if they didn't agree with them. During the second semester the FYP college was frustrated with the inactivity of its president, who had never really wanted to be an officer and who never called meetings. The college elected one of the two women who had originally wanted to be president. The football player who had threatened the professor for talking about feminism applied to become a CA in the FYP the following year, knowing he would have to promote reflection on gender issues as part of his job.

This is a perhaps overly optimistic account of the kinds of bitter conflicts that occur among diverse members of campus communities, conflicts that faculty, ostrich-like, usually fail to see, but it is also illustrative of the educative processes that can evolve through struggle and critical reflection on what it means to respect people for and despite their differences.

It is clear now that these issues cannot be adequately addressed in any curriculum, course, workshop, or year-long program. Indeed, the experience with the FYP suggests that even when faculty and staff commit to working with these issues in an integrated, comprehensive effort, the progress that can be made is always mitigated by failures. But if even a program like the one at St. Lawrence dredges up and in many cases exacerbates tensions and conflicts stemming from diversity, one has to ask who is being served by programs that ask *less* of students and faculty. It could be argued that one-shot diversity requirements, either curricular or co-curricular, enable administrations to say that they take seriously the issues of gender, cultural diversity, and democratic pluralism while students and the student culture are left effectively unchanged. In the following section we will examine some cases drawn from our practice. They suggest that although the architecture of the FYP enables a kind of engagement with difference superior to that of traditional educational designs, that architecture promises more than it can deliver.

An Experiment in Social Contracts

Charged with integrating the curriculum and co-curriculum so as to foster democratic community, the original faculty of the FYP devised an approach that was formal, elaborate, creative, and doomed from the start. Each FYP college was to engage in a study of community and to practice self-government by creating a social contract. We agreed to a curriculum that included Aristotle, Hobbes, Locke, Rousseau, and Marx, feminist and radical critiques of these theories, and at least one non-Western perspective on the relationship between individual and community. The project was then to ask students to use these theories to analyze critically their lives together in the residence halls. The product of these deliberations was to be a constitution or contract, collaboratively and democratically produced, which would govern their communities.

Assuming that many of the social ills of college life arise from a combination of anti-authoritarian rebelliousness and the many biases that students bring with them, we believed that allowing students to create their own rules and their own ways of dealing with conflicts would encourage them to reevaluate their attitudes and behavior. Although some of the contracts produced were complex and insightful, in more than three dozen experiments over three years, none of them was ever implemented, employed, or appealed to in any kind of sustained way. These failures were nevertheless educationally useful, as they engendered grounded reflection on issues of participation, alienation, and apathy.

The failures of the social contract taught us that the goals—of getting students to reflect critically on their lives together; of getting them to engage their differences openly, fairly, and productively; of getting them to participate in the communities in which they were ostensibly members—would call for strategies that were much more agile, specific, and informal than this original design. The general strategy that followed, and that has proven much more effective, has been for the faculty and staff of each FYP college to pay constant close attention to how their colleges are evolving, in the class and out. We have found that seizing particular issues in the colleges and working on them with the students has brought us closer to our goals and has shown us in more detail the depth and difficulty of those goals.

Collaborative Governance in the FYP

Crucial here are issues of leadership in democratic communities. In the early years of the program, most colleges sought to develop community through strong leadership. Whether exercised by the faculty, by the upper-division students who live in these communities as college assistants, by the students who emerged through elections or dynamics of popularity, or by various coalitions of the preceding, community development and governance was tightly held by a few who invested a great deal in their work. Our experience confirms Benjamin Barber's thesis that strong leaders make for weak citizens. Barber argues that "a too responsible leadership can make for an irresponsible citizenry; an overly vigorous executive can reduce citizens to passive observers whose main public activity is applause. Public officials displaying an omnicompetent mastery of their public responsibilities unburden private men and women of their public responsibilities and leave them with a feeling of civic incompetence or civic indifference" (1993, p. 163).

We have found that when faculty or students, acting from their commitment to the goals of the FYP, tried to realize those goals through their own work and will, the majority of the students were utterly disenfranchised from the process and alienated from the community. Our goals statement asserts that we aspire "to promote critical reflection by students on values, identity, and difference, to encourage students to move toward patterns of living together which reflect principles of mutuality, accountability, and respect for difference, to encourage students to develop a sense of themselves as individuals able to assert rights within the context of social responsibility" (Statement of Philosophy, 1993).

Especially in cases where gender or cultural or racial differences precipitate tensions or conflicts, the implementation of these goals demands a kind of guidance that Barber calls "enabling leadership" (1993, p. 166). As enabling leaders, faculty and student staff in these instances act as "guarantors of equitable participation" (p. 166). Their role is not to solve the conflicts, contain the tensions, or render differences invisible, but to attend to the forms of their engagement. Recalling Dewey's commitment to communication in the development of democratic communities, Barber states that the task of enabling leaders is "to ensure that participants in the political process listen as well as they talk, or that the usual talkers are made to listen, and the usual listeners get a chance to talk" (p. 168).

The residential life of our FYP colleges is rife with tensions and conflicts that are instances of or analogous to the major divisions in our society. Students regularly negotiate over the use of bathroom space, and these negotiations are thoroughly laced with issues of gender, culture, and class. There are always students who are morally offended by how others use language, alcohol, or drugs. There are deep differences in how students explore and express their sexuality, and these differences can divide the colleges. In the early days of the FYP, faculty and student staff, acting as "strong leaders," would rush into these conflicts, deconstruct them by invoking sophisticated theories, and in so doing disempower and disenfranchise those involved. We have learned to approach the complicated lives of students with more humility, and we realize that real change, real growth, and real education are fostered not so much by resolving tensions and conflicts as by trying to ensure that the parties involved communicate with one another with as much respect and empathy as possible.

Rarely do parties enter into conflict from equal positions of power. Part of our job in working with intentional, integrated communities is to ensure that the communication we encourage does not simply reproduce or mask existing social inequalities. We have to be vigilant and must educate our students to be vigilant about the ways dominant patterns of discourse and dominant modes of social interaction act to perpetuate existing inequalities. Thus the staff and faculty of the FYP try to identify and support students in situations where they would not easily be able to enter the conversations as equals. But having provided that support, we expect all participants to take on the tensions of uncomfortable, mutual efforts at understanding and respect.

Reframing Roommate Conflicts in a Diverse Community

In one recent case, a white student from the rural North Country arrived at St. Lawrence to discover she had been housed with an urban, African American student. Her parents immediately called the dean of the first year to complain that their daughter was very anxious about this situation, that the two students were too different to be comfortable roommates, and that we must change the housing assignment immediately, or they would pull their daughter out of school. In traditional academic structures a situation like this would be handled by student development staff and counselors, who would approach it as a private matter to be handled therapeutically. The goals of the intervention would be to minimize the conflict and to work with the two students involved to resolve "the problem."

Approaching this roommate complaint as a private matter would leave unrecognized and unenjoined the educational and social dimensions of the situation. The tension was not between two individuals, who had not had sufficient interaction to make judgments about one another. In fact, the white student told members of the FYP staff that her anxieties were not about the black student per se. She protested that the black student "seemed really nice" and that she "didn't want to hurt her feelings" but the black student was just "so different that she didn't feel comfortable being in the room with her." The white student was judging on the basis of stereotypes about racial and cultural difference, but it is important to add that the stereotyping was bidirectional. The African American student stereotyped the white student as a North Country racist. The point is that this situation needed to be engaged by positioning it within the larger social and political context that created it. In other words, much of what the FYP is about was in play and on the line the very first day.

The second dimension of the complaint that would be missed in a traditional approach is that situations like this rarely unfold as strictly private matters. In this case, the white student immediately sought the counsel of other North Country students she knew, and it seems as though the idea of demanding a room change came from the advice of her upper-division friends. The African American student, who had been on campus for a precollegiate summer program and was therefore well connected with a number of first-year and upper-division students of color, sought their counsel. These students, who as a group are politicized and well organized, approached the FYP with their own set of concerns. Once the narrative of the situation entered the public domain, it took on a life of its own. Very quickly the protocommunity of the FYP college was discussing the matter in groups small and large, and the college was headed toward a very early disintegration into factions taking the side of one student or the other.

The faculty of the college, who knew of the situation immediately because they serve as the advisers for their first-year students, contacted the student development professionals associated with the college. Together they sought a meeting with the dean of the first year, who is responsible for the First-Year Program in toto and whose primary responsibility is to facilitate the thorough integration of academic and student affairs as they pertain to the lives of first-year students. He in turn called a case conference involving the faculty and student development staff of the college and consultants pulled in from other offices of the university, based on their areas of responsibility and expertise. Together they collaborated in planning strategies of intervention. The dean talked with the parents of the students and tried to invest them in the educational potential of the situation. The faculty advisers, together with the student development professionals, met with the roommates individually to listen to their concerns and to try to provide a context for critical reflection on what had happened and how they felt.

The faculty and staff also convened a meeting of the college as a whole and tried to pull forward a discussion begun during orientation about diversity and democratic community. The night new students arrive they attend a performance of an adaptation of Studs Terkel's *American Dreams* (1980), in which upper-division students perform dramatic monologues representing American cultural diversity. The next morning, in their FYP seminars, the students discuss the performance and are then asked to write a personal narrative in which they reflect on their situation vis-à-vis "the American dream." That discussion was available to the faculty and staff of this college to work with as it related to the situation at hand. In other words, they could engage the students in a critical analysis of their current and very present experience in a way that did not reduce it to personalities and quick moral judgments but instead placed it in its social, political, and historical context. Here were students engaged with the tensions of diversity in democratic community development, not merely as they are represented in books and arguments but as they were being negotiated in real time and with serious personal investment by most members of the college.

Everyone did not live happily ever after. The outcomes of this were not enduring harmony, deep lessons learned once and for all, or anything of the sort. The white woman chose to stay enrolled in school and in the course, but to live at home. The African American woman enjoyed her double room as a single and had a successful semester. The college still had many of the predictable conflicts and negotiations. But the structure of the FYP afforded a kind of teaching and learning in this case that is not typically available. Again, the work of this program does not show how diverse, democratic communities can be formed within the academy as much as it illuminates both the complexity of the issues and how skeptical we should be of courses or workshops that purport to do more with less.

What we can take away from the experiences of St. Lawrence's First-Year Program is that Dewey's goal of education for democracy is extraordinarily challenging in a society crisscrossed with multiple layers of inequalities and differences. Dewey was right to insist on communication as the basis for associated living, but he was wrong to assume that those entering the conversation should have to speak from the master's subject position in the master's words, with the master's body language. Because the means and the mode of conversation are part of what needs to be negotiated, neither communication nor community can exist prior to the other. Community can form only through finding a means for communicating, and communication can occur only through the interactions and interdependence entailed by recognition of community. None of this will happen easily. College campuses ought to offer safe spaces where people can experiment with diversity in community, but often their adherence to elite traditions of academic culture or, lately, their accession to consumer demands, inhibits the kind of open, committed participation in intercultural negotiation that diverse communities require.

If this society is to move toward full participation, everyone is going to have to reexamine assumptions about what the rules of communication are and how they can be adapted to fit different speakers. As our experience with the FYP shows, this will not happen through a workshop or a course. It is a full-time, ongoing commitment to Deweyan praxis, to a continuous feedback loop of theory and experience. Formal education can introduce students to the issues and to some experiences of how differences in identity, race, gender, ethnicity, or class actually affect epistemologies and manners, thus preparing them for a lifetime of communicative praxis. As Dewey himself said in *Democracy and Education*, "We are far from realizing the potential of education as a constructive agency for improving society" ([1916] 1966, p. 79).

Chapter Five

Learning Communities

Collaborative Approaches
to Engaging Differences

Roberta S. Matthews, Daniel J. Lynch

These are not easy times for higher education. Like all large public, city, or state institutions, LaGuardia Community College of the City University of New York faces the challenge of decreasing money and services at the same time as student enrollment, particularly of those with special needs, is increasing. We know through the work of Astin (1993), Light (1990, 1991), Tinto (1987, 1994), and others that the best academic experiences are small and personal, and promote as much interaction around academic issues as possible between faculty and students. As resources get tighter, however, the natural impulse is to simplify and homogenize, to seek procedures and activities that may be universalized, to move toward large, simple, cost-efficient solutions that have interchangeable parts and people.

At LaGuardia we see each day that we do not have interchangeable parts and people. Our students look different from us and from each other. We serve a remarkably diverse group of students. Demographic projections anticipate that by the year 2000, 50 percent of City University students may be classified as English as a Second Language (ESL) students. Currently at LaGuardia, 40 percent of our students classify themselves as Hispanic, 26 percent as black, 18 per cent as white, and 16 percent as Asian/Pacific

Islanders. Although approximately 10 percent of our eleven thousand matriculated students are visiting foreign students who come from ninety-six different countries, many of our regular students are the children of immigrants or are immigrants themselves. Our students collectively speak more than forty-five different languages. Similar to other port-of-entry cities scattered along the coasts of the country, we are both enriched and challenged by an influx of present and future citizens from all over the world who often arrive unable to speak to us or to each other. The common denominator must be created, not assumed.

Daily we face the challenge of forging "a new kind of community which honors our multiplicity" (Guarasci and Cornwell, 1993, p. 7). Gail Green, a member of the LaGuardia English department, suggested in an interview with the authors the degree to which diversity is at the center of our experience: "I'm not sure there's any other place in the world where the conversation about 'difference' has the urgency that it has in New York City. It's an extraordinary thing that we all are in classrooms together; no matter how much one talks about the mix of life in New York City, we often live in segregated communities; frequently, students have said to me how incredible it is to find themselves together in a learning community as much as they are, talking about very volatile subjects. . . . [The] opportunity to talk about difference through the materials we use is a powerful situation."

Many of our students are graduates of inner-city high schools; their experiences are the antithesis of our vision of a good education. At the 1994 American Association of Higher Education School/College Collaboration conference, keynote speaker Linda Darling-Hammond eloquently spoke of our most stressed students spending their high school years in large institutions, with 3,500 to 4,000 other students whom they neither know nor trust. Here they are exposed daily, in large classes, to six or seven different teachers, none of whom know their names, for forty-three-minute sound bites of fragmented information. When she concluded, a member of the audience leaned over to a colleague and whispered, "and if they are *real lucky* they'll go on to the very same type of institution of higher learning." Clearly, this type of experience does not foster the thoughtful development of skills and abilities that contribute to academic success or that prepare students to be future citizens in a democratic society.

At LaGuardia, we use many approaches to humanize and enrich education and to use it as a vehicle to create community. In this chapter we will focus on two of these approaches: (1) learning communities that promote collaboration among faculty members from different disciplines, and (2) active, collaborative learning practiced within these communities or in individual classes throughout the college. Although they cannot fully compensate for increasing class size, learning communities and collaborative learning can provide the small, personal, intense academic experiences that support students, increase retention, and promote success. In addition, they provide an environment in which students acquire the skills and the confidence to participate in the intellectually challenging and difficult dialogues that need to occur in the nation today.

Learning Communities and Collaborative Learning

Learning communities are conscious curricular structures that link two or more disciplines around the exploration of a common theme. They can be designed as paired courses, as clusters of three or more courses that constitute the entire course load for students, or as "coordinated studies" groupings that serve as the entire educational experience during a given semester for both the students and the faculty involved. Learning communities facilitate increased communication around shared interests among faculty, students and faculty, and students themselves.

Collaborative learning occurs when students and faculty work together to create knowledge. At its best, the collaborative classroom "provides a social context in which students can experience and practice the kinds of conversation valued by college teachers"

(Bruffee, 1984, p. 642). Collaborative learning embraces a variety of active learning approaches that value the voice and contributions of all participants. The process welcomes students into the academic community, and functions as a context for the considered and reflective interchange of ideas. The collaborative classroom promises "to turn the conversation . . . into a [multiplicity] of voices—a heterogeneity without hierarchy" (Trimbur, 1989, p. 615).

We focus on learning communities and collaborative learning because they are educational approaches that support and move forward the democratic agenda. In 1916, John Dewey asserted that "a society which makes provisions for participation, in its good, of all its members on equal terms and which secures flexible readjustment of its institutions through interaction of the different forms of associated life is in so far democratic. Such a society must have a type of education which gives individuals a personal interest in social relationships and controls, and the habits of mind which secure social changes without introducing disorder" ([1916] 1966, p. 99). By providing a context for "different forms of associated life," learning communities and collaborative learning help us forge community out of difference. They allow us to acknowledge diversity while seeking commonalties. They provide the means to balance the needs of the students who compose our community while enabling each to develop Dewey's essential "habits of mind." We believe that our experiences may serve as a model for other colleges and universities seeking to create community out of difference as well as for those that are seeking to introduce "difference" through curriculum if little exists in the student body itself.

The History and Practice of Four Programs

In this chapter we will describe four models of collaboration among faculty and students at LaGuardia Community College: liberal arts clusters, Enterprise and the Coordinated Freshman Programs, New Student House, and the COPE program. We view these from several perspectives: as curriculum writers, as participants, and as administrators involved with the programs over the years. We seek to provide an overview of their history and design, and some insights into the human interactions that make them work. These programs draw their strength from the active participation of faculty and students, bolstered by the active support of key administrators. Our discussion thus depends heavily on the comments and observations of faculty and students who were interviewed for this chapter in 1994. This will be a chapter of many voices.

The climate and values of higher education are changing. The recent attention being paid to collaborative and cooperative learning and the proliferation of learning communities on campuses across the country reflect a new focus on the importance of teaching and learning. More than two hundred American colleges and universities are sponsoring some type of learning community, and faculty in probably twice as many institutions of higher learning are experimenting with collaborative and cooperative learning in their classrooms. Nevertheless, both students and teachers have long been conditioned to respect the boundaries of their relationship, and they approach any change or apparent transgression very gingerly. We do not advocate intimacy or "palship" with our students; instead, we celebrate our relationship with them and with other teachers in a collaborative, intellectual effort that enriches the academic experience for all involved.

The Liberal Arts Cluster

Learning communities formally began at LaGuardia in 1979 as required introductory clusters for day liberal arts majors. They are a group of courses centered around a theme chosen by the professors. All students take all courses in the cluster.

The cluster always includes a three-credit college composition course and a two-credit course called "Writing the Research Paper." There is also a one-credit "integrating seminar." Two other three-credit courses fill out the cluster, often an introduction to sociology and a liberal arts elective that might cover such topics as an introduction to philosophy, oral communication, the history of New York, or computers and society. The creation of clusters is faculty driven. Instructors seek out kindred spirits and recruit likely colleagues. They then go with their proposals to the department chairpersons and the office of academic affairs in the springtime to formalize their plans. Each year, LaGuardia runs eleven liberal arts clusters serving three hundred students.

Coauthor of this chapter Dan Lynch, who has frequently taught in liberal arts clusters, describes the writing courses and the "integrating seminar" common to all clusters. As we write this, he is teaching, and often team teaching, in a cluster called "New York, New York" with Ming Yan, a sociologist, and Richard K. Lieberman, a historian.

The composition course offers the opportunity to use collaborative techniques involving the use of computers and peer critiquing. From the first day, students are encouraged to think of writing as a process, one made up of the prewriting, drafting, revising and editing, and proofreading stages. In almost all the writing courses, students use computers with word processing software to write their essays; they work in labs where each member of the class has access to a computer. On a physiological level, the video screen helps students concentrate on their writing. While the students are working on their essays, the teacher uses the time to meet with students on an individual basis for conferences on their writing, generally on the task at hand.

For more than a decade, the English department has been using small-group peer critiquing to involve students actively, to reinforce the mutuality of the learning process, and to help students understand how a manuscript goes through stages. While becoming writers, students become readers and editors of each other's work, although the writers only gradually accept each other's authority as readers and editors. As they develop their peer critiquing skills, students plunge into each other's lives, looking to their colleagues as resources for help (as opposed to competitors) and thus seeing the world from startlingly new perspectives. Dan Lynch describes an experience that suggests how collaboration helps those engaged in the learning process to hear each other's voices:

> One day, fumbling to illustrate some point I was making, I used a tired cliché: "as certain as death and taxes." Who's going to argue that? Up shoots a hand. One of my students, a very articulate African American young man, caught me up short by saying that he wasn't going to die. Say, what? I needed to get into this.
>
> "What do you mean you're not going to die?"
>
> "Just that. It says in the New Testament, 'There are those in this generation who will not see death.' Christ will come and establish His kingdom. Society as we know it will come to an end, but the world will continue and we will be living on it." He said these words as confidently as he might have said, "There are those in this generation who will collect Social Security."

The other students jumped on this and questioned him closely. It turned out there was yet another student in the class who belonged to the same sect but to another Brooklyn congregation. She shared his confident views that death was not necessarily for them. This illustrates an important point: if I cannot assume a common ground with two of my students even on our mutual mortality, all of my assumptions about shared perspective can be asserted only tentatively, at best.

Later in the semester, in a segment of the course given over to oral reports, the young man discussed his beliefs with the class and the perspective they gave him. The other students asked if they could visit his church. He said he would welcome them but that they should be prepared for the minister, who sometimes said outrageous things. The student had on more than one occasion, along with other members of the congregation, "taken the minister to the Scriptures" to prove a point about which they disagreed with the minister.

What this remark suggests about the nature of the student's relationship with his minister indicates that the student is part of a democratic religious community in which the participants discuss their views openly. His willingness to speak up initially, to challenge Dan's "certain as death and taxes" remark, and to explain his views to the class is related to the community from which he came, where he was accustomed to challenging the traditional authority embodied in the minister when he disagreed with him. There is a clear link between the community the student belonged to at home in the church and the community he belonged to in Dan's classroom.

We who are the skeptical children of the Enlightenment must be aware that we are inviting into our learning communities those who may center their lives on faith and scripture, be they the Torah, the Gospels, the Koran, or the Bhagavad Gita. Asking such students to acknowledge the value of intellectual diversity and multiple cultural and ethical perspectives can be for us and them a painful challenge.

At the very moment a student's core beliefs in culture, class, gender, and sexual orientation are being challenged, when he or she is looking for some stability, it is vital that the teacher be there. Looking for models or perhaps certainty—in the text, in the teacher, in one's classmates or one's more senior fellow students— the student encounters only questions. The teacher can be demanding and must have clear academic standards, but a democratic, Whitmanesque sense of respect and equal worth must be evident in the spirit of the classroom relationship. When you shake up students, you have to be there when they start to stumble and flail around. Working with colleagues and students collaboratively in the environment of a learning community helps faculty see themselves as learners alongside their students. As power relationships shift, it is easier to hear and acknowledge different voices.

In the "New York, New York" cluster, Lieberman and Lynch made arrangements for extensive team teaching in the research paper course, concentrating on documents relating to the Harlem riots of August 1943: newspaper accounts; letters from residents, bigots, union leaders, political office holders, and religious leaders; internal police memoranda; property damage reports; radio transcripts; oral history on tape and film—all made available by the LaGuardia-Wagner Archives, which are located on campus and directed by Lieberman. A nationally known urban historian, he showed the students in one team-taught lesson what he does when looking at a document such as a letter from an angry citizen that the mayor received after the riot. Lieberman is able to articulate very clearly and with considerable humor what goes on in his mind as he asks himself questions about a document. This modeling encourages students to be bold about looking for avenues of research on their own that they will develop into a formal research paper in the writing class.

Clearly, the cluster promotes the exchange and exploration of different points of view. Thus, the team-taught integrating seminar of the "New York, New York" cluster has the theme of "perspectives." Throughout the cluster, time is spent honing student appreciation of multiple perspectives. Ming Yan and Dan Lynch distributed a list of questions that the students use as a script or algorithm for analysis. The questions, derived from material developed by the Coalition for Essential Schools, are used as tools for understanding:

1. What is the other person's (author's, speaker's, or historical figure's) perspective? What forces possibly shaped that perspective? Can we explain the perspective in sociological terms (for example, class or values)?

2. What is the relationship of the event, the argument, or the idea to economics, politics, law, technology, psychology, or especially sociology or history?

3. What verifiable evidence is provided?

4. What if the situation were otherwise? How can we change the situation, if necessary? What is our first step? Final goal?

5. So what? What is the event's relevance to me?

6. What is its relevance to humankind?

In the seminar, with the help of these and other questions, faculty seek to model how individuals from different backgrounds and academic disciplines may perceive, analyze, discuss and disagree over an issue:

> I [Dan] remember the shock that ran through the class last year when Dr. Joan Greenbaum, a professor of computer science who was team teaching the integrating seminar with me said, "You're wrong, Danny."
>
> The students fell silent and were perfectly still in their chairs. "Uh-oh," you could hear them saying to themselves. In their worlds, women didn't tell men in public they were wrong. In academic situations, of course, they do; everyone does it to everyone else. It's a key element of the search for truth. It's part of the game. We went on with our discussion.
>
> I said, "No, I'm not."
>
> She said, "Sure. Let me tell you why . . . ."
>
> And she did, and I said, "Well, if you're going to look at it that way, yes, I could see why you might think I'm wrong, but what I was trying to get at was. . . ."
>
> It was a very conventional academic conversation, no big deal. But the students started to breathe again, as if their parents had stopped fighting and things in the house were back to normal.
>
> Joan caught this, and during the week she brought it up, saying, "We have to go back to them with this and talk about it. This is important. They need to know men and women can disagree, that there are ways to do it. That it's OK. That it's even necessary." We did, and the students made "disagreement" one of the skills the class practiced.

In terms of planning collaborative efforts, it is important for teaching teams to be diverse so that different perspectives naturally emerge and students can see this happening. So many of our students come from fractured backgrounds that we must supply opportunities for them to act out whatever yearnings they have to be part of a community.

Our classrooms are a safe haven. In a democracy, people can disagree without killing. This is not necessarily true in the street. During the first week of the new semester, the students in the "New York, New York" cluster were given one minute to write anonymously about their most important experience or observation at LaGuardia thus far. Here are three responses:

> I'm impressed by the variety of teachers and students of different race and color. I am amazed that kids actually want to learn and teachers actually like teaching. Also, I'm impressed with the maintenance of the grounds and freedom to walk about without somebody searching your bookbag for guns and drugs.

> When you start a discussion, it's great how different ideas from everyone can make you understand a topic better and see it differently from what you initially thought it meant.

> There are obviously different nationalities and cultures. We must have been brought up in different ways. But I consider personalities. So, I'm curious about their thoughts. Do they think about the meaning of life?

We think we see three students, wide-eyed and willing, on the verge of committing themselves to being part of a democratic learning community. And we know, from past experience, that the cluster helps initiate them into the academic community by giving them the skills, the confidence, and the support to accept the challenges of future coursework.

Enterprise and Coordinated Freshman Programs

Enterprise, begun officially in 1990, evolved from an earlier failed attempt to create a minicollege for students in business and computer majors. Its development provides a case study of one approach to unifying faculty and securing from them enthusiastic, committed involvement.

Enterprise offers students a variety of course pairs and clusters that link career with developmental skills or liberal arts courses or both. During a typical year, six hundred to eight hundred students elect to take pairs and clusters sponsored by Enterprise. For example, a developmental math course is combined with an introductory course in computers; an ESL course for students with good math skills is linked with both a transfer computer science course and a career-oriented introduction to computers course; an introductory business course is linked with courses in economics and composition. During 1993–94, summer and academic year programs for new students, which receive outside grant funding, were combined with Enterprise. Currently, Enterprise and Coordinated Freshman Programs have evolved into the "place" where new learning communities find support for development and implementation.

Enterprise emerged from the following circumstance: by the mid-1980s, LaGuardia was losing 30 percent of its first-year students before the beginning of the second quarter. We had a retention problem. Studies showed that although there were "positive" reasons for the loss, such as transfer to a senior college or placement in a full-time job, the overwhelming majority of those questioned reported that they had no sense of belonging to the institution. They were isolated, didn't know the names of their professors, and saw no connections among the various disciplines they were studying. LaGuardia was in danger of becoming the kind of large public institution that Linda Darling-Hammond described in such devastating detail a decade later. The students who voted with their feet cut across all skill levels: the most able were leaving at the same rate as the least able. Because 70 percent of LaGuardia students majored in one or another business program at this time, the three departments that served these students—accounting/managerial studies, computer information systems, and office technology—became the focus of attention.

The president felt that the college should develop a minicollege within the larger college and eliminate the "haphazard" curriculum by creating clusters of courses for these students. A faculty committee appointed by the department chairpersons met and designed the Center for Business Careers and Values (CBCV). The name suggests the battle associated with the initiative: liberal arts faculty asserted the need for values education, the business faculty the need for career education. Meryl Sussman, director of Enterprise and Coordinated Freshman Programs, discusses the creation of the original program: "In retrospect, it is clear that CBCV was viewed as a mandate coming down from on high. By the end of the first year we knew the model was not going to work primarily because of faculty resentment. Faculty had been told to teach in a cluster, but they had no idea how to do it, nor did they know how to do the collaborative, active learning that was, after all, at the heart of the program."

We began to think about the problem of isolation among the faculty. Many college faculties, divisions, and departments are not second homes to their members. Political or personal differences, arguments over standards and syllabi, turf wars, and (real or perceived) racial, ethnic, gender, sexual orientation, or class differences may create an atmosphere reeking of rancor and backbiting, with nothing but curt nods in the hallway and a collective sprint to the parking lot or subway at the end of the day. Moreover, those teachers who are solitary by temperament may withdraw from contact with colleagues outside the classroom. They may look forward instead to sharing experiences and engaging in worthy dialogue only with those specialists within their own fields, those who attend the same conferences.

In "Collaborative Learning Comes of Age," Zelda Gamson (1994) deplores the general absence of a sense of cooperation in higher education and suggests that we need to establish a cooperative spirit in order to address the issues currently facing higher education: "The collective life of higher education is deeply flawed today. A sense of community is hard to find anywhere, even in small colleges. Collaborative projects among faculty often fail. . . . The gap between faculty and administrators grows wider as resources shrink. . . . Life in departments is often an exercise in parallel play. . . . A more collaborative culture would help enormously . . . a more collaborative culture is a precondition for solving other problems facing higher education" (p. 49).

Such a powerful metaphor as that of the isolated scholar, self-justifying servant of truth, may do college teachers a disservice. If their primary task is teaching, maybe they would be better off working with their fellow teachers. They might be more effective, the experience might be invigorating both emotionally and intellectually, and the climate of the college might be improved. David Damrosch in *Lingua Franca* (1995) notes that "specialization has its virtues, but its triumph has led to a 'patterned isolation' of academic life and work . . . and this patterned isolation has serious consequences: it inhibits collaboration and breeds alienation and aggression throughout the university" (p. 60). He suggests that neither is necessarily bad, citing the careers of scholars who by virtue of their stance have made important contributions to society. Nevertheless, he ends by observing that "the university's ethic of alienation and aggression has bred isolated and peripatetic professors, estranged from their colleagues on campus and from the communities in which they live" (p. 60).

If, as the editors of this book argue in Chapter One, "it is likely that the mutuality and reciprocity necessary for democratic order will minimally be undone by this other prevailing need for difference" and that traditional visions of democracy must be replaced with "a wholly different ideal of the democratic community in which both difference *and* connection can be held together" then it is in ourselves and in our classrooms that these changes must occur. In an interview with the authors, Meryl Sussman traced how this type of evolution was facilitated by Enterprise:

In 1989 [coinciding with a change in the administration of the college], we decided to offer a faculty seminar in issues of higher education, student development, learning communities, collaborative learning. We invited a "guest list" of fourteen faculty to participate based on such questions as "Who is innovative? Who is not afraid of taking risks? Who is senior faculty and might be ready to do something different? Who normally works intimately with students and does not prefer the lecture model?" Roberta [Matthews] designed and facilitated the seminars. My job was to make matches as we heard faculty talk about their problems. The pairings emerged organically, and that was the breakthrough because the faculty saw purpose in the clusters.

Such faculty seminars can help transform the "ethic of alien-ation and aggression" that Damrosch sees as all-pervasive on our campuses and that Guarasci and Cornwell characterize as a threat to our survival as a democracy. What began at LaGuardia as one attempt to address a local problem and to salvage a failed program has evolved into an ongoing offering by the office for academic affairs, a series of seminars whose content responds to needs expressed by faculty and staff. The seminars were originally facili-tated by Roberta Matthews, who repeated during five subsequent quarters the original seminar on issues in higher education and stu-dent development with an emphasis on learning communities and active learning strategies. Although in hindsight it would be easy to assert it as our original intent, it was actually somewhere along the way that we realized the seminars were yielding a cadre of fac-ulty and staff throughout the college who could be turned to with confidence whenever new initiatives needed support and staffing.

By the end of the original cycle, almost eighty faculty and staff from all over the college and from our two high schools had partic-ipated. In response to participants' requests, in 1992 we also offered a couple of "advanced practicum" seminars on collaborative learn-ing, which resulted in an in-house publication, *Notes from the Field: Reflections on Collaborative Learning at LaGuardia* (Matthews and Associates, 1994b). During a "multipurpose" seminar in fall 1993, small focus groups identified two areas of need based on surveys they had conducted as part of the seminar: the orientation and integration of new faculty and the orientation and integration of new students. To address the latter, Meryl Sussman, working with colleagues across the college and using grant moneys from the Coordinated Freshman Programs, created "First Step," an all-day event in late summer that introduces five hundred of our new students to our academic programs and includes a financial aid workshop, advisement, and early, painless registration. To address the needs of new faculty, a group of faculty met in spring 1994 to develop case studies about teaching at the college (Matthews and Associates, 1994a) that were then used in fall 1994 as the centerpiece of a seminar for new faculty facilitated by the chairperson of the professional development committee of the college senate.

In fall 1995, the "Creating Community in a Pluralistic Classroom" seminar was facilitated by a faculty member from our human services program who has a certificate in conflict resolution. Seminar content and approaches evolved from a series of meetings with several faculty and staff at the college (including the assistant principal for guidance of our Middle College High School), all of whom had expertise of one kind or another in conflict resolution. Before the summer break, the designated seminar participants met in a full-day meeting to brainstorm possible directions and to identify their own needs. The seminar provides members of our community with the opportunity to articulate and examine issues that arise from our particular situation. Each participant has committed himself or herself to bringing the process back to his or her own departments, in the hopes that the conversation will inform and enrich our practice throughout the college. At LaGuardia, the professional development seminars have become a flexible mode of responding to current interests and issues and of generating products, suggestions, and solutions that have an impact on the larger community in one way or another.

Meryl Sussman suggested another advantage to this model:

Faculty participate in Enterprise and the Coordinated Freshman Programs activities because they love meeting faculty from other disciplines. Faculty can get to be so insular, it's nice to have lunch with someone from another discipline. But [learning communities are not] for everyone. We only use volunteers; it's deadly when a faculty is told "you have to do it this way." We have faculty who love to participate in our seminars but say "I'm not going to teach that way, it makes me too uncomfortable; others say "this is what I've been looking for". . . .We sometimes decide not to offer a successful pair or cluster again if the faculty who developed it are really not able [for workload reasons, for example] to teach it and we cannot find comparably skilled and interested substitutes. We also cut our losses quickly; if a learning community does not come up to our standard, we withdraw support. We focus on quality, not quantity.

As ideas emerge for new learning communities, the office of Enterprise and Coordinated Freshman Programs facilitates their creation. Potential combinations of courses are evaluated to make sure that student populations are available to them. Whenever possible, pairs or teams of faculty initially receive one hour of released time to develop a joint syllabus. Eligible students are targeted for special mailings or special registration to ensure that the learning community will fill and run. In myriad ways, the office thus supports and expedites experimentation and collaboration.

The existence of the office of Enterprise and Coordinated Freshman Programs has been a valuable resource in light of recent rapid and dizzying changes in financial aid regulations, credit allocations, and budget cuts, which all have impeded the ability of our students to begin and complete their education. As chairpersons and faculty develop new combinations of courses for our ESL and basic skills populations, they have an office and an individual to turn to in order to confirm the existence of target populations, identify the potential of new combinations of courses, and facilitate the creation and offering of new learning communities. As we reach beyond the boundaries of ESL and skills courses to combine them with content courses, our track record reassures the academic area that standards will be maintained because we have the data to support the idea that faculty who consciously work together and actively involve students in the content of their classes will accomplish considerably more than those who work alone. We are struggling to maintain access to higher education for our students; we know we can only succeed by working together.

New Student House

New Student House, developed during the 1991–92 academic year and piloted in 1992, was designed based on an earlier model, the Supercluster, created for students with multiple basic skills needs. New Student House transformed that cluster, which served a small number of students, into a coordinated studies model that brings together developmental reading, writing, speech communication courses, and counseling for a much larger cohort of students (sixty-six to ninety per semester, depending on grant funds available and the exigencies of whatever current fiscal crisis exists at the time). New Student House generally provides participating faculty with a full workload.

Originally funded by a three-year grant from the state of New York, the New Student House team was able to spend a year planning and meeting at least once a week from January to June. Brian Gallagher of the English department served as the creative genius and able administrator of the effort. Each participating teacher was released for three hours over two semesters for planning, curriculum development, and project design. Participating faculty all stress the importance of the planning period, which gave them the precious time to come together as a group to work their way thoughtfully toward the unifying theme of "relationships" and to create the links between the courses. Will Koolsbergen, one of the faculty participants, noted in an interview: "I've taught in collaborative ways with other faculty where I've not been this successful. I think what made this group successful is that three very flexible instructors are willing to listen to one another and try to come to a true collaboration on how to approach a topic or a theme." Koolsbergen also pointed out that in addition to facilitating various interdisciplinary links, the innovative structure allows for various kinds of rein-forcement: "When students come together in groups of ninety in the theater [the biweekly joint three-class meeting], they quickly see what they have been doing in the thirty-person class is very per-tinent to the rest of their lives. And that's very beneficial. If I were teaching three separate sections of speech, I wouldn't get that kind of link and the immediate student gratification."

The program was successfully implemented the second year. During the third year, the original teaching team—Sam Amoako (communication skills), Michael Horwitz (counseling), Will Koolsbergen (speech communication), and Phyllis Van Slyck (English)—committed to training two additional teams so that the population served by New Student House could be expanded. Cur-rently, the college offers three New Student Houses annually, serv-ing 120 to 160 students.

The thematic link for New Student House is a study of rela-tionships; the rich set of readings, activities, and writing assign-ments reflects the variety of student backgrounds. The curriculum is a model for the kinds of contents and approaches that create a new kind of community that honors student multiplicity. As Phyl-lis Van Slyck explained in an interview:

We made a joint decision to explore issues of cultural diversity. For example, we had the students read Ali Ghalen's A Wife for My Son and we discussed it in all our classes. It's a novel about an arranged marriage. It connects with the conflicts between French and Alger-ian culture. . . . We all come from a background that is not totally fixed. Identity is part of a dialogue. There are things that can be changed. . . . We were discussing a scene in class. It's the young cou-ple's wedding night and he takes her very, very forcefully, and all his friends are outside yelling and the women are going "lillillillilllll" in the way Arab women have. So this Brazilian young woman stands up [in class] and says, "This is outrageous! He raped her!"

A Chinese woman says, "On the contrary, he is being a good husband and a good son."

Then the Brazilian says, "How would you like to be raped on your wedding night?"

The Chinese says, "We are better . . . in our culture they see each other before they marry."

I intervened, "We shouldn't use 'better than they are' statements. Everybody thinks they're better. Be a little more self-reflective."

It was a very intense moment. Cultural diversity . . . it was right there.

Intense involvement on the part of faculty and students comes with a cost, but for thoughtful participants, that cost includes valuable lessons about themselves. Phyllis Van Slyck articulated the evolving nature of the process:

What do I think about it now? After doing it for a few years? The intensity can be draining. Energizing, but over the long haul, it's tough. I'm maybe a little tired right now of race, gender, and class issues. It's painful for the students and for the teachers. You have to deal with all these hurt, angry feelings. I'm trying to develop topics and strategies that are less direct and deal with important issues without putting students on the spot. For example, in a faculty workshop recently, a colleague reported on an exchange in which a student said, "Politicians only care about Jews."

"So," the instructor asked, "why do you think that may be the case?"

The student replied, "Well, maybe Jews vote more." You can go a lot of places with that. It was a less volatile approach.

As faculty learn how to survive the difficult contexts and to complete the difficult tasks they have set for themselves, they offer their students the opportunity to succeed in college. During the first year of working with students who historically had a dropout rate that hovered around 40 per cent, New Student House lost only one student from the original seventy-five. Subsequently, New Student House students have continued to maintain an impressive record of course completion and retention. In an article written for an in-house publication on collaborative learning, Michael Horwitz contrasts the experiences of students in New Student House with those who were not part of the learning community: "I realize how few [non-House] students I still see as compared to students who were involved in the House. I believe one of the reasons is, for some of these students, the New Student House offered some vague form of stability. . . . Even though the New Student House is only a title for a program that in reality has no identifiable locale on campus, it is quite possible that it provides some sort of temporary shelter from a world of ignorance, poverty and violence" (Horwitz, 1994, pp. 66, 69). Structures such as New Student House are rescue operations, reaching out and providing students with the support they need to become functioning and contributing students and citizens.

COPE

The Career Opportunities Program for Employment (COPE) is a holistic, integrated program whose implementation provides a particular group of individuals with an opportunity to become their best selves. Sponsored by the Human Resources Administration of the City of New York and aimed at providing educational opportunities to (primarily) women on public assistance with children (who receive support under the category of Aid for Dependent Children, or AFDC), the program was inaugurated in spring 1993 and currently serves more than 550 students. According to the program categories under which ethnicity is reported, 36 percent are black non-Hispanic; 45 percent are Hispanic, and 19 percent are white non-Hispanic. Because it was begun after the other programs we have described, COPE was able to take advantage of our institutional wisdom of practice.

The COPE program incorporates learning communities as part of an intensive first-semester immersion in collaborative classroom environments. New Student Seminars are integrated into each learning community and taught by one of the two COPE counselors assigned to work with these students for their entire academic career at LaGuardia. There is also a first-semester career development seminar and a COPE job developer who places students who graduate or who leave the program. Students have access to tutoring labs throughout the college and a special COPE tutoring area. They participate in supplemental instruction initiatives offered through the office of academic affairs, and in advisement and registration activities that combine resources to guarantee a thoughtful and efficient program of classes each semester.

The students respond to such treatment by staying in college and moving toward graduation. COPE has a retention rate of over 70 percent; 40 percent of COPE students consistently maintain a GPA of 3.00 or higher (out of a possible 4.00). Graduation rates exceed the 30 percent goal by the end of two years that was articulated in the original proposal. In addition, during the 1994–95 academic year approximately fifty students were placed in full-time or part-time jobs. A comment from a course feedback form eloquently states the importance of COPE in the lives of its participants: "Without COPE, people who want to achieve a better and higher status in life would not be able to leave their lives of doom. COPE is an inspiration to people. It saves people's self-esteem and helps people to believe in themselves again. COPE is like a family. It is always there for you when you need it most."

Above and beyond the statistics and the data, COPE succeeds because of the individuals involved in the program. Under the leadership of Audrey Harrigan-Lamont, the program continually finds new ways to work with its students, who are supported in their efforts to navigate between their household obligations and their college responsibilities. With the help of the teachers and fellow students, they manage to muster and maintain the energy and commitment necessary to meet the demands of college life. The dynamics of student life in COPE provide a safety net for women who might otherwise be in free-fall. Here are two COPE students discussing the dynamics of the group:

> *Linda Graham:* There are maybe fifteen people in the cluster and at any given time I will have ten calling me on the phone, maybe because I am the oldest. . . . I am the mother figure. . . . The majority of the class is between thirty and forty and then there's me, and a couple who are eighteen, nineteen, twenty who we fuss at constantly. . . . I just fuss at them in class, and when class is over I fuss at them more.
>
> *Interviewer:* Why do they keep calling you?
>
> *Linda Graham:* I guess they just like to hear me fuss at them.
>
> *Gina Richard:* No, it's not that. It's the wisdom.

COPE students appreciate the impact the experience has had on their self-esteem, self-confidence, and self-image. Although this manifests itself in the kind of interaction noted here, it also results in another kind of interaction noted by Linda Graham: "With two of our professors [in the cluster], we can talk to them about anything. They are like family. But we had a little problem with one in the beginning . . . the whole class had a problem and we gave him a cold shoulder. It wasn't an organized effort. He got on everybody's nerves, he treated us like kids, so we decided 'we're not speaking to you, see how you feel.'"

In a sense, both of these interactions come from a common collaborative experience. Interpersonal issues are part of the territory in any cluster. Students who spend extended amounts of time with each other and with their teachers are empowered to articulate and act on reactions that most often do not surface in traditional, stand-alone lecture courses. This makes the lecture a "safer" model for a faculty member, but a less active and involving experience for both faculty and students. Especially in today's climate, the lecture does nothing to counteract the impact of the popular talk shows, where apparently ordinary people are comfortable sharing the most intimate details of their lives and their innermost feelings with millions of strangers in exchange for the opportunity to have advice shouted at them from the audience or called in from around the country. Partly because these shows provide an (inappropriate) model for group discussion, it is rather easy to get a discussion going in class. The challenge is to establish a respectful context, raise the level of discourse, and insist on the use of verifiable evidence and sources. Structured collaborative small and large group discussions assert the importance of content quality and help ensure participation with knowledge.

In the instance described by Linda Graham previously, the professor knew what was happening in his class and was sensitive to the need to discuss it with his students. The situation became an opportunity for a conversation about assumptions and expectations. Maureen Doyle, another teacher in the same cluster, commented in an interview on the evolution of the class over time:

> Early on, the class was fragmented, people off on their own. Now they are moving to a common understanding of what is acceptable and what is not, of what we can tolerate from individuals and what people won't tolerate from others. There's a sense of tolerance around hearing different things and the behavioral issues are resolving themselves. People are coming together and working through difficult issues where we all may have different perspectives. Something really good is happening. . . . I've had perfect attendance for the last three sessions, which meet in a block of three and one half hours each week. That's a long class.

College life has opened new doors of opportunity for women on public assistance who are recognizing the connections between education and employment and are exploring career options as part of their educational experience. The COPE program exemplifies the finest kind of public education that a democratic society can offer its citizens. However, instead of becoming a model of good practice, a program like this is now an endangered species; it will most likely disappear in the current political climate.

Conclusion

We have described programs and approaches that promote academic success and make a difference in the lives of our students. When results are unsatisfactory using traditional approaches to higher education, critics often blame the shortcomings of students themselves or their prior educational experiences. Participating in learning communities and practicing collaborative learning are predicated precisely on the notion that the problem resides not in the students but in rigid and antiquated pedagogical structures. It is in the students that we find the genesis of the solution, not the origin of the problem. Catalyzing students as a positive force occurs when sufficient avenues are opened up for an ongoing and variegated dialogue conducted across disciplines and equally among students, among teachers, and between students and teachers.

Sociologist John Hyland assesses the value of such experiences: "[When I teach in a cluster] I'm taking into account what other people are teaching; there are themes beyond my course, so it stretches me—it's more difficult. The students have other experiences they bring to class, and I am trying to make those connections in my own mind. The cluster does communicate to the students the notion that this is an important way to learn—to connect, to go across and see that the disciplines are different aspects of the whole, not totally distinct and separate." In his interview, Hyland described a traditional stand-alone class in which teacher and students were engaged in reviewing the causes and effects of the French and Indian Wars. He observed, "I don't think they had a clue about *why* they were doing this at all. There was a whole layer of assumptions underneath that didn't get addressed. I would have a problem working in this way. The cluster, on the other hand, contributes to the notion of connections, of articulating assumptions and the relatedness of material."

In *Collaborative Learning: Higher Education, Interdependence and the Authority of Knowledge* (1993), Kenneth Bruffee characterizes

students as "outsiders" and asserts the value of collaborative learning in college classrooms: "[Students] enter their classes ignorant of
the community-constituting language that the teacher speaks. . . .
Much of what college and university teachers say sounds to students, as Rorty puts it, either kooky or revolutionary. . . . The
importance of collaborative learning is that it acknowledges these
differences and creates conditions in which students can negotiate
the boundaries between the knowledge communities they belong
to and the one the teacher belongs to" (pp. 123–124). Collaborative learning, because it is based in the social construction of
knowledge, assumes that there is a bridge between our students'
home communities and their college communities. The practice of
collaborative learning helps students cross that bridge.

The experience of Gina Richard, a student in a successful cluster course, illustrates the notions of connectedness and relatedness
so important in a learning situation. Assigned materials developed
by the American Social History Project about Irish immigration in
the 1840s to the Five Points tenement neighborhood in Manhat-
tan, the class worked collaboratively with the content: "When we
studied the Five Points material [in the COPE cluster], we broke
into small groups to discuss what we saw. . . . There were lots of
similarities: unions, gangs, segregation, substance abuse, child abuse
and child labor laws, homelessness. The only difference was the
time frame. There was a lot to relate to and learn from." As students become insiders, they integrate materials and perspectives
that initially might have been foreign to them.

What each of us perceives and acts on as "true" has much to do
with our "situation"—social, political, cultural, religious, or philosophical. If the "truth" is socially constructed, then all members of
any group who are engaged in a search for "truth" need to have a
clear notion of how our situations or identities affect our views.

The LaGuardia classroom is particularly challenging because
with its extraordinarily diverse population, these situations are mul-
tiplied. Labels not only don't tell the whole story, they are not even
especially descriptive. For example, the students introduce them-

selves on the first day of the new semester: "My father is Dominican and my mother is from Haiti, but they're divorced, so sometimes I live with one and sometimes the other. I'm thinking of moving in with my girlfriend and our son. She's from the Philippines." Or one student might say she's Greek and so might another, but the first is a just-arrived Cypriot young woman from a hillside village and the other is third-generation from nearby Astoria, into thrash rock, and has a buzz cut and some major tattoos. Their identities are complex, resistant to quick pigeonholing.

For any particular student, her situation or identity is never stable but rather always in flux, moving along a continuum from what she was to what she will be (and occasionally reverting or switching direction) depending the student's age, the stage of development of her personality, and the intensity of her desire to "become educated" or "to become an American" or "to discover who she really is" and leave what she was behind.

The wonder of it all is that human beings can decide to change who they are. Teachers at LaGuardia watch students grow aware of this freedom, and it is like nothing else, short of witnessing a birth. "You mean I don't have to be this?" No. "I can be that?" Yes. And then they become.

The diverse, collaborative, democratic learning community is a place where change can occur and where it can be nurtured and supported. There are hardly ever any violent moments and rarely much overt hostility arising out of differences in "situations" in our classrooms. The students themselves don't view diversity as a problem. In fact they value it, citing it in various feedback mechanisms as one of the most attractive features of their experience at LaGuardia.

A democracy is a place with many perspectives; anything that helps its citizens understand that only makes it stronger. Our students learn that there are perspectives different from theirs. They learn this in many ways, whether by reading a challenging text by a strong writer or by listening carefully to their fellow students. To say, "Yes, you think differently from me. Yes, let me listen to you and think about what you say, and maybe I will change." That is the defining act of democratic dialogue. But it is hard to achieve.

It is clear that democratic dialogue often does not come easily. As we listen to faculty voices in this chapter—from the social sciences department, the natural and applied sciences department, and the English department—they speak of whole layers of assumptions that don't get addressed, of working through difficult issues when we all may have different perspectives, and the pain of dealing "with all the hurt, angry feelings." The challenge of breaching the barriers to democratic dialogue transcends particular disciplines and taxes the skills and training of individuals. The graduate education of most college faculty rarely addresses how one ensures an environment of civility during the discussion of controversial topics; how one encourages breadth of vision without descending into chaos; how one practices tolerance in the context of affirming essential values instead of abandoning them; or how one asserts the necessity for compassion and cooperation in the face of inequity and inequality.

Even among ourselves, we find it hard to work together to address the social and educational tasks that confront us; it is even more complicated to facilitate conversations around these issues among our students. Yet it is precisely that dialogue upon which the conversation of democracy depends. Faculty who are immersed in learning communities and collaborative learning are compelled to explore and experiment in the context of difficult dialogues with colleagues who share their experiences and support their efforts. In this situation, faculty may celebrate the diversity of their students and acknowledge the variety of communities from which they come, but they must at the same time articulate the common assumptions and values that will foster and enrich our democratic traditions.

As educators, it is our responsibility to collaborate with our colleagues and our students to ensure our survival as a civilized society. Phyllis Van Slyck underscores the advantage of teaching in an environment that honors diversity and values its potential for creating community: "I think it's a real advantage in an urban community college setting to have people of so many backgrounds represented. It makes it pretty much impossible for one group to dominate or intimidate another. In class, we have ten different languages spoken at home. That's a lot of ways to say good morning." Thus the democratic spirit is nurtured.

Chapter Six

Intergroup Relations, Conflict, and Community

David Schoem

One of the tests facing America and American democracy is how best to utilize difference and conflict in ways that are beneficial to the development and sustenance of communities. America has cherished, even idealized, the notion of community, but it has not wanted to recognize the inherent conflict that exists within pluralistic communities and a pluralistic society. The University of Michigan's Program on Intergroup Relations, Conflict, and Community (IGRCC) is built on the belief that institutions of higher education can assist students in exploring models for building community while acknowledging differences between and within groups and recognizing the complexity of individual and social group identity.

Intergroup Relations, Democratic Citizenship, and Liberal Arts Education

The IGRCC program is based on the belief that one of the goals of a liberal arts education is to advance students' knowledge and understanding of diverse peoples and lifestyles. Such an agenda requires new curricular and co-curricular programs that forthrightly and vigorously seek these goals—through intellectual inquiries, experience-based reflections, and joint tasks and projects. This program offers an initiative in undergraduate education to advance students' knowledge and awareness of diversity; to assist students' exploration of the relationship between social conflict, community, and social justice; and to increase students' skills in responding to intergroup conflict and divisions within their own university community.

Cornel West (1994a) writes that the challenge facing America today goes beyond racial conflict and group divisiveness to the very survival of American democracy. He argues that American democracy cannot be sustained as a democracy that is for some Americans but not for all, and that the growing economic and political disenfranchisement of so many Americans poses a critical challenge to this democratic society's future. Higher education, through programs like the one described in this chapter, can respond to this challenge to democracy by developing citizens who are well educated, who are prepared for a diverse democracy, and who desire to be active and knowledgeable participants in a diverse democracy.

The IGRCC program is structured so that intergroup conflict and community building is addressed within the context of the university's mission to provide its students with a liberal arts education. In this way, the university legitimizes and incorporates this agenda within its central intellectual and academic programs (Guarasci and Cornwell, 1993). Thus it is not the provision of a service to a particular group or groups that underlies this program, but the broad education of the entire undergraduate community.

Given the current level of intergroup ignorance and distrust in the United States generally and in our secondary educational systems in particular, intergroup conflict on personal and institutional levels is a natural and pervasive phenomenon in the nation's universities. Intergroup conflict points to the need for more attention to be given to building community and coalition. Overt campus conflict as well as more subtle campus climate concerns also reflect our failure to teach young people how to resist and overcome societal divisiveness and how to build communities that manage and use conflict for socially constructive purposes. A meaningful and systematic effort to educate students about racial, ethnic, religious, and other conflicts requires giving students the skills and understanding to strengthen a democratic society that will recognize common purposes among its peoples while at the same time accepting and mediating valued differences. The study of intergroup relations is best served not under the circumstance of crisis between racial and ethnic groups, but by scholars' and students' looking to texts and social interactions from which to develop conceptual frameworks and models for practice.

Although overt tension may occur in the undergraduate student community, it is an analytic error to see this as a student problem; it is a problem all members of university communities face, and its roots are located in the structure and culture of universities and the larger society. Faculty and administrators should not be surprised that they face a major educational problem—how to teach young people to use social diversity constructively for personal and intellectual growth and as a laboratory for making democracy work in a pluralistic environment.

The Michigan approach to intergroup relations is multifaceted. In addition to providing an intellectual grounding, the IGRCC program offers students skills in conflict management and community building. It provides students with personal experience in structured conversations—intergroup dialogues—across racial, ethnic, and other social group boundaries (American Commitments National Panel, 1995b). In doing all of this, the IGRCC program gives students both the academic background and social experience necessary for informed participation in a diverse democracy. These areas of content and skills are taught through academic courses and extracurricular groups offered in a partnership of the College of Literature, Science and the Arts, the office of the vice-president for student affairs, and the office of the vice-provost for academic and multicultural affairs.

As initially launched, the program was called the Program on Intergroup Relations and Conflict, a title that did not explicitly emphasize the critical link between community and conflict. Its new focus and new name—the Program on Intergroup Relations, Conflict, and Community—was implemented and given widespread attention on the University of Michigan campus in winter

1995. The College of Literature, Science and the Arts and the Program on Conflict Management Alternatives organized a "theme semester" on the very topic of conflict and community, bringing together faculty teaching more than twenty-five affiliated courses, a public lecture series, a film series, and two new courses on this topic offered through the programs in American culture and women's studies. As a result of the strength of this conceptual approach, that year the university's commemoration of Martin Luther King, Jr. Day was organized around the theme "Conflict and Communities."

Program Description

Although it is curriculum based by design, the IGRCC program is also by intention one that is fully integrated with the student affairs division. This partnership between academic affairs and student affairs is unique for large public universities, and it is essential for helping students fully understand issues of intergroup relations, conflict, and community. The program director(s) are supported by an advisory board composed of faculty from the departments of American culture, psychology, sociology, and women's studies, and key administrators from the College of Literature, Science and the Arts, and the offices of the vice-president for student affairs and the vice-provost for academic and multicultural affairs. It has served approximately three hundred to five hundred students annually through course offerings and co-curricular activities.

The program now offers four major areas of learning: (1) academic courses, (2) face-to-face intergroup dialogues, (3) student leadership development and staff training, and (4) workshops. The program also plans to begin developing a fifth major area of learning, off-campus retreats, for the following purposes: engaging in intensive study, reflection, and dialogue with advanced students; providing introductory workshops for high school students and entering college students; and experimenting with building intentional multicultural communities and coalitions.

Academic Courses

The academic courses provide students with disciplinary and inter-disciplinary understandings of intergroup relations, conflict, and community with faculty from American culture, psychology, sociology, and women's studies working in collaboration and teaching a variety of courses. The academic component of the program includes first-year seminars, sophomore and upper-division courses, community service learning courses, and minicourses (American Commitments National Panel, 1995a). The first-year seminars are courses linked together as Freshman Interest Groups (FIGS), variously offering common lectures, films, assignments, and occasional team teaching. These courses average approximately twenty-five students each. The seminars were created to replace a large 100-level lecture course on intergroup relations primarily because experience showed that the small size and discussion format of seminars were more conducive to active engagement with the intellectually difficult and complex topics that were fundamental to the course. The upper-level courses are intended to build on the seminars with more advanced readings and critical analysis. The community service learning courses provide students with an opportunity to access this content area through yet another learning modality that also provides local communities with desired services. The minicourses emphasize skill development or a special focus on a particular area of intergroup relations. The following are examples of the specific courses within each category:

- First-year seminars
  Topics on "Intergroup Relations, Conflict, and
  Community"
- Sophomore-level and upper-division courses
  American Culture 399   "Race, Racism, and Ethnicity"
  Sociology 401   "Social Change and Intergroup Conflict"
  Sociology 410   "Ethnic Identity and Intergroup Relations"

Psychology 401   "Special Problems—Psychology of Ethnic Identity"

Psychology 401   "Special Problems—Conflicts and Coalitions in Pluralistic Communities"

Women's Studies 231   "Introduction to Women of Color and Feminism"

Women's Studies 260   "Differences Among Women"

- Community service learning courses

  Psychology 201   "Project Outreach"

  Sociology 389   "Project Community"

  Women's Studies 350   "Women and the Community"

- Minicourses on intergroup relations, conflict, and community (courses vary and have included those listed here)

  "Resolving Conflicts"

  "The White Experience in a Multicultural Society"

  "African American and Asian American Relations"

  "Intercultural Communication"

- Intergroup dialogue on conflict and community

  Psychology/Sociology 310   "Training in Processes of Intergroup Dialogue"

  Psychology/Sociology 311   "Practicum in Facilitating Intergroup Dialogue"

  Psychology/Sociology 122   "Intergroup Dialogues"

Intergroup Dialogues

The face-to-face intergroup dialogues are a unique feature of the IGRCC program. They represent an opportunity for people from different backgrounds and cultural identities to learn about each other's histories and experiences, to challenge stereotypes and misinformation, and to address issues of intergroup and intragroup conflict and community building in constructive ways. IGRCC describes intergroup dialogues as follows:

> The primary goal of an intergroup dialogue is to foster deeper under-standing among groups by exploring attitudes, feelings and percep-tions of one another—in some cases this simply means developing a better understanding of the reasons for disagreement and conflict. Another goal is to create a setting in which students will engage each other's intellectual and emotional selves in open and con-structive dialogue, learning, and exploration. Intergroup dialogues provide students with the opportunity to learn from each other across social group boundaries, to challenge one another and them-selves as they consider alternative viewpoints, and to actively seek more just resolutions of social conflicts. As such, intergroup dia-logues serve as an important building block toward the develop-ment of multicultural educational communities on college campuses [Program on Intergroup Relations and Conflict, 1993].

Intergroup dialogues consist of ten to fourteen participants and are coordinated and led by two trained student facilitators—one from each of the two participating social identity groups—who help foster a safe setting in which participants engage in dialogue and address substantive issues in a meaningful way. They use a small-group, semistructured discussion format. Short readings and experientially based activities are incorporated to encourage dia-logue and discussion of pertinent issues. Some intergroup dialogues are open to all students, whereas others are affiliated with a partic-ular course or student organization. There are twelve-week and six-week intergroup dialogues offered on a wide range of issues, such as "People of Color and White People," "Men and Women," "Chris-tians, Muslims, and Jews," "Latinos and Latinas," "Gays, Lesbians, Bisexuals, and Heterosexuals," "International Students and U.S. Students," "Asians and Asian Americans," "Blacks and Jews," and "Latinos and Blacks."

Training

An intensive training program is provided to graduate and undergraduate students who facilitate the intergroup dialogues. High-quality training requires faculty involvement and oversight from the development stage through training and supervision of practice. Skilled leadership of these groups is essential, given the students' level of discomfort with and even fear of engaging peers from different backgrounds in discussion of long-avoided, potentially explosive issues. Without a well-trained facilitator, attempts to enter into dialogue across racial, ethnic, gender, and other group differences are likely to result in the emergence of ill-managed and potentially destructive conflict. The program also provides more general staff training on intergroup relations to student staff who work in student affairs offices (housing, orientation, and so on).

Workshops

The IGRCC program also offers one-time workshops to students to address particular topics and concerns. Student organizations, student governments, fraternities and sororities, and the like periodically ask the program to make presentations on various aspects of intergroup conflict and community building. The program occasionally organizes film series, special lectures, and interactive programs in conjunction with other campus events.

Program History

The IGRCC program began in 1988 with funding from a competitive undergraduate initiatives grant provided through the offices of the president and provost of the University of Michigan. Subsequent funding has come from a variety of university offices, including the College of Literature, Science and the Arts, the student affairs division, the associate vice-president for academic affairs, the vice-provost for academic and multicultural affairs, the Pilot

Program, the psychology and sociology departments, and the housing division.

The initial program concept was derived through a partnership of the Pilot Program and the Program on Conflict Management Alternatives (PCMA), bringing together the complementary resources of an innovative, residential undergraduate academic program with an interdisciplinary research and development faculty team, respectively. The Pilot Program brought to the partnership significant experience and success addressing the concerns of minority undergraduate students and responding to intergroup conflict in a living-learning environment. For a number of years the Pilot Program had offered courses on intergroup relations, such as "Blacks and Jews: Dialogue on Ethnic Identity" and "Israeli and Palestinian Dialogue," courses with a focus on underrepresented minorities and groups facing conflicts, courses addressing attitude change, and out-of-class discussions and "rap sessions" on black-white relations.

PCMA, funded by the William and Flora Hewlett Foundation, is dedicated to the work of seeking cooperative techniques to manage conflict by exploring links between social structure, social justice, and conflict resolution. The PCMA faculty, composed of distinguished faculty from six different colleges and schools at the University of Michigan, constitute an interracial, cross-gender, cross-status team of scholar-activists. The assumptions and concerns underlying PCMA's agenda fit the need of the university community with regard to education about intergroup relations, conflict, and community. These concerns are as follows: (1) for understanding social justice and injustice as "causes" or "criteria" for assessing outcome, (2) for promoting long-term change in the organizational relationships and social structures that give rise to escalated conflict, to support new ways of working with conflict, and (3) for institutionalizing these alternative approaches.

Subsequent to the initial funding period, the program continued to expand and gain student, faculty, and administrative support. However, its funding base still relied on outside funds.

Later changes in the administrative leadership of the Pilot Program and the departure of the core (untenured) instructor for the large introductory classes left an imbalance on the academic side of the program partnership that was developing between academic affairs and student affairs. The student affairs division lent more permanent funding to the program, which helped to sustain and revitalize it in the interim. Most recently the program has restructured and strengthened its academic and intellectual component, rethinking its core introductory course, expanding course offerings, and providing for greater faculty involvement and oversight and closer integration between the academic and student affairs components. There are now plans to seek external funding to improve and intensify the training of student coordinators of the intergroup dialogues, enhance the first-year seminar FIGS, develop off-campus retreat opportunities, and increase dissemination of the program activities and outcomes.

Practice and Discourse

The recurring comment made by students who participate in the program is about the impact of participating in substantive discussions with peers from backgrounds different from their own. That this stands out as the most apparent achievement of the program is a remarkable commentary on the seemingly impenetrable social barriers of American society. Students today come from communities more segregated than they were thirty years ago, and increasing numbers have no skill or experience with others (Massey and Denton, 1993).

Crossing Boundaries

As one member of the program faculty put it, "Students are not really choosing to be separate, but there is no vehicle to cross boundaries. This program provides a safe and continuing structure to discuss issues." In the words of two student participants, as cited in Zuniga and Nagda (1993):

> Without this program, I could have gone the entire semester without talking to a minority student [p. 236].

> As a White man do I want to talk to a Black person about racism? It can be really scary. I feel like a dialogue group is really a safe place for people to talk about difficult issues. We can sit down and can talk about these issues and learn [p. 236].

European American students in particular are least likely to have had substantive contact with people who are not European American. It also comes as a shock to many African American students who have grown up in segregated communities to live in a residence hall in which they do not represent the numerical majority. An outside observer might think that social interaction would be easy and commonplace when these and other groups of students arrive at a campus whose student body comprises so many different backgrounds. In fact, such interaction rarely occurs.

> I never had such a deep discussion with people of the opposite race before. I never actually realized how many misconceptions people of the White race have about minority races [student participant, cited in Zuniga and Nagda, 1993, p. 237].

> We wave "hi" to the African American students on our hallway but, frankly, we haven't said a word to one another all year. It's amazing. And the same pretty much holds true for all the other groups of students. A lot of people are just afraid of being different [student participant, cited in Zuniga and Nagda, 1993, p. 237].

Fear of difference is an attitude our students have learned throughout their lives, without any apparent contrasting societal model (Schoem, 1991). It is probably the primary inhibitor of dialogue and interaction across groups. There exists little or no incentive or structure for students to interact substantively with people from different backgrounds. The IGRCC program, however, by providing a safe structure for discussion on more than a one-time basis, offers students a vehicle for crossing these boundaries of separation. Some students come to explore issues, some come just for the opportunity to have a friendly conversation. But all students want to hear the stories of their peers, and they enthusiastically return for more dialogue once they realize that the stories they tell of themselves will be listened to by the others in the room.

> I went in thinking the discussion would be focused on the other students. But at the end of the term I heard many people saying "I've really learned a lot about myself" [student participant].

> The first time I went I wanted to see what it was like just because there's so much segregation at this school. But after the first dialogue, I felt so lucky to have gone; I just learned so much [student participant]!

Public and media discourse on diversity and multiculturalism has narrowly framed the issue as a power struggle in which one group seeks to gain some advantage at another's expense. What students with such apprehensions quickly learn in this program is that such need not be the case. These dialogues encourage sharing, active listening, and learning about oneself as well as about others.

> Some students think separatism is positive, that it is a necessary step to better understanding one's racial/ethnic self and surviving in a dominant culture [program faculty member].

The students with the attitude mentioned in the preceding quotation view separation as a survival strategy rather than as a hostile or negative act toward another group. When this point of view is raised in the program's dialogue groups, it creates considerable tension and disappointment. At the same time, this view causes students to think deeply about the experience of different groups and the different attitudes of individuals within each group.

One of the most important lessons students learn from these discussions is that just as there is often a bonding among members of any given group, no group is monolithic, and intragroup differences are evident in every case.

> Our definitions of democracy and difference need to change. Today they seem to be seen as separate, but we need to understand the interrelationship of democracy and difference [program faculty member].

The IGRCC program is as much about societal change and citizenship education as it is about individual learning. For American democracy to hold together requires that its rich diversity be cherished and honored. The citizenry must acknowledge the common values it holds across group differences. Students participating in this program are practicing democracy as they identify commonalities across their different backgrounds and build a community of trust as they talk through difficult questions. They embody the interrelationship of democracy and difference in their course or multiweek intergroup dialogue commitment to explore their racial, ethnic, religious, and other group experiences together and to work through conflicts and differences that they identify.

> I personally was not as interested in identity issues and intergroup relations. Now I ask myself all kinds of questions. My roommate and her friends have no interest in these discussions. A lot of my friends are happy where they are. They have their same-interest friends. A lot of people are so afraid of being different still. Like being somewhere where someone is different than you is the worst possible thing. A lot of people have their lives set. They believe that the way they think is right and that's it [student participant].

As successful as the IGRCC program is, there are many students on campus that it does not reach. Although the program does have a presence on campus, the dominant paradigm on campus and off remains one of separation and division. It is simply too easy, even on the floor of a diverse residence hall, to ignore students who come from different racial, ethnic, and religious backgrounds or who have different sexual orientations. It is far easier to maintain friendships exclusively within one's own group even if it means making invisible whole populations of people or ignoring the individual student living right next door. "Having been offered multiple lenses to view social realities, [students] are able to go beyond thinking about 'you and I' to memberships in social, cultural, economic, and political groups and the subsequent impact on the 'you and I' relationship" (Gurin, Nagda, Lopez, and Sfeir-Younis, 1993).

Preliminary research conducted on the program indicates that students in the introductory course developed a more complex understanding of intergroup conflict, moving from a strictly individualistic perspective to a more general understanding of structural causes of racism, inequality, and societal divisions. Thus, although students do recognize the opportunity for change based on individual responsibility, they now also see the institutionalization of power differentials.

Managing Conflict, Building Community, and Training Leaders

According to the program director, "The program has created a special cohort that has lifted itself beyond typical assumptions and stereotypes—these students have moved beyond the wall of separation to ask important, probing questions and to step in to effectively address conflict." Students participate in a fifty-hour training session as part of their preparation to facilitate intergroup dialogues, and each year the program has increased the quantity and intensity of the training in recognition of the difficulty of the task. These undergraduate and graduate student facilitators have participated in the program and have demonstrated academic and social leadership in intergroup concerns. Their training prepares them to facilitate intergroup dialogues, but these students also represent an at-large core of skilled conflict mediators on campus as well as a cohesive group of students who practice "boundary crossing." As issues of conflict and community arise in residence halls, fraternities and sororities, student clubs, and racial and ethnic groups, these students stand out as the ones who are not only comfortable with difference and conflict but are also skilled in using conflict to work toward constructive agreements and community building. They become the educated citizenry of the university campus, actively participating to make a diverse student body a truly effective student community.

> As a result of my participation in this program, I feel much more comfortable dealing with conflict and much more willing and capable of confronting my friends when they make racist comments [student participant].

> [The training course] taught me to value different ways of thinking and different ways of interacting. I've especially been thinking about different cultural styles of interacting and how clear that was in the Black-White dialogue; how the White people were working on one set of rules and the Black people seemed to be working under a different set of conversation rules . . . just became really fascinating to me. And I really learned . . . how to see all of those as good and valuable in and of themselves; what's really bad is when one style or cultural way of interacting is set up as the norm that everyone else has to follow [intergroup dialogue facilitator, cited in Nagda, Zuniga, and Sevig, 1995, p. 387].

Those students who are participants but do not become intergroup dialogue facilitators also report an effect in terms of wider campus impact. These students state that they engage these issues with their peers, are more likely to attempt to broaden their circle of friendships with peers from diverse backgrounds, and also assertively confront fellow students about contested statements and actions. They are more willing to intervene in conflict believing there may be a constructive resolution; they feel less threatened by conflict and feel more comfortable with disagreement than they did previously.

You're dealing with hard issues. You're dealing with things like racism and people's feelings about this. And it's not like if they don't read a chapter in anthropology class; they'll get that next year, or they won't learn it . . . so what? But if a dialogue group goes badly, it makes a big difference [intergroup dialogue facilitator, cited in Nagda, Zuniga, and Sevig, 1993, p. 398].

Intergroup dialogues can go badly. As this chapter has pointed out, students come to these discussions with fear of difference, distrust of conflict, and inexperience with dialogue. Add undergraduate student facilitators to this mix, and the potential for things not going as desired is considerable. Dialogues can fail for a number of reasons. If there is a climate created that is not safe for openly discussing issues, then students will speak little more than clichés and nothing will be learned. If a safe climate is created but then students are not helped to discuss effectively the sensitive issues that are raised, then there is opportunity for comments to be misinterpreted, for comments to be hurtful and left unaddressed, and for comments to be shared without context and outside the group. Another problem can result from an imbalance in the number of people representing different groups. In such circumstances, the dialogues become more one-way presentations rather than true interactive dialogues.

To reduce the possibility of dialogues not working as planned, there is, in addition to the fifty hours of training for facilitators, close supervision of the dialogues-in-progress by consultants who work closely with the facilitators, and there are debriefing meetings of the facilitators as a group. Furthermore, there is an active recruitment process to reach out to prospective participants so as to offer a balanced number of participants from each represented group.

Teaching with Innovative Pedagogy

Because the study of intergroup relations and conflict cuts across many of our current social and behavioral science disciplines, such courses are necessarily interdisciplinary in character. In order to be maximally effective, they must employ an innovative pedagogy. Courses are relatively small and place an emphasis on a transactional and experiential pedagogy, on the discovery of students' own experiences and attitudes, and on the examination of the campus and community environment as well as the consideration of primary scholarly resources. As one student participant put it: "You have to come and share ideas—that's a *real* curricular revision." Abstract intellectual material is a part of these courses, but these courses also ask students to examine their own cultural ignorance and intolerance or to analyze and counteract the ignorance and intolerance of others. Such courses take place on the campus and in the community. Because a high level of student-faculty interaction is required for this type of instruction, a premium is placed on recruiting faculty members who are committed to the practical goals of addressing issues of conflict and community as well as to the intellectual study of these issues.

These courses were initially housed—literally and figuratively—in the context of a living-learning program. That association allowed the intentional bridging of content and practice to occur: the integration of classroom theory with the social experience of the residence hall. Today that association continues, but the program has broadened its outreach to students throughout the campus.

> I think the greatest thing about the classes is that they offer an unorthodox forum to hear people speak and think about other people's experiences. It also helped me challenge what I felt and helped me formulate my own views. Because it personalizes issues [student participant].

An instructional program that seeks to transform or educate young people beyond their cultural ignorance and intolerance must take advantage of two principles of adult learning: (1) that educational interactions should be focused around real and immediate issues and experiences, ones that have a direct impact on the lives of those involved and in the organizations or communities of which they are a part; and (2) that instruction should be transactional in character, replacing unilateral transmission of instruction with joint inquiry by co-participants. In these settings, and according to these pedagogical principles, rich conceptualization and effective reflection on scholarly and theoretical principles and materials can be best developed and used (Schoem, Frankel, Zuniga, and Lewis, 1993).

The aim of advanced courses is to provide advanced intellectual and practical instruction in techniques of preventing, reducing, or negotiating disputes and building community. Attention is given to various targets of individuals' learning: knowledge, attitudes and beliefs, interpersonal and organizational skills, team-building strategies, problem solving, coalition forming, and change making. In addition to their immediate intellectual as well as social growth, students gain skills that prepare them for graduate programs in law, business, public health, social work, and in many related careers.

> I can't tell you how much I learned. I came out of every dialogue feeling like I knew so much—and it was from each of the individuals there talking. There were a lot of personal issues I learned in the dialogue, but the class was much more general and theoretical [student participant].

A pedagogical paradox of the IGRCC program is that during the time students participate in both a program course and an intergroup dialogue, they often have difficulty recognizing the linkage between the two. There is no question but that the two are integrally linked, and it indeed has been the intention of the program to offer the theoretical in conjunction with the more personal. Yet it appears that the immediacy of the more personal intergroup dialogue experience is so powerful that it is not until sometime after completing both the course and the intergroup dialogue that students are fully aware of the powerful intellectual connection between the two. When students do realize the connection, it is rewarding to faculty to see how students use the intergroup dialogue to inform their theoretical understandings and bring the theory to inform their personal dialogic conversations. Yet it is also frustrating and challenging to faculty at the time of the experience to hear students talk about a course and an intergroup dialogue that are intentionally interconnected as though they are very separate learning activities or to have students resist writing papers that bridge the theoretical and the personal.

Crossing Boundaries as an Institution

At the University of Michigan, the Program on Intergroup Relations, Conflict, and Community has found support from all sectors of the university community—administration, faculty, and students. It has received funding from units as widespread as academic affairs, student affairs, and multicultural affairs. However, as much as program participants recognize and cherish their broad support, they continue to negotiate program institutionalization and funding.

The success and imagination of the program stem from its being rooted in many sectors of the university. The issues that this program addresses do indeed require a holistic approach, one that extends beyond traditional boundaries of student affairs and academic affairs. At the same time, this kind of programmatic boundary crossing is highly predictive of institutional fragility and uncertainty at campuses across the nation (Boyer, 1987). Although active goodwill prevails among all the interested parties, the gulf in institutional structure and practice at times makes program life feel precarious in this university borderland. One visitor noted that these types of programs seem to "hang by a thread."

The program has faced these friendly but unsettling fissures on a number of occasions. For instance, after an initial round of funding from the president and provost, it was necessary for the program to find a more permanent home or homes. All of the interested parties quite reasonably required buy-in from their institutional counterparts. What stood in the way, however, was that there exist no easily replicable models on which to build. At different times academic affairs or student affairs has taken the lead in program development and leadership, with their counterpart properly looking on to assure that an even balance is maintained.

For a program on intergroup relations, conflict, and community, these difficulties are improbably metaphoric. A society that is constructed along structural divisions—in other words, one whose citizens remain socially, politically, and residentially separated along racial, ethnic, religious, and other group divisions—is certain to face difficulty focusing on common interests and the common good. The society will be hard pressed over time to sustain democratic principles; conflicts will be exacerbated, and efforts at community building will be difficult to achieve. Although the IGRCC program works to confront these societal divisions in the service of developing effective participants in a diverse democracy, it struggles against structural divisions within the university community that serve to make more difficult this very activity of the program.

> It would be unfortunate if the program were seen as a "firefighting" unit that would dampen all student conflict around intergroup relations, and it would be just as unfortunate if such a program were seen as a "staging" arena to alter the university's stance on matters of intergroup relations [program faculty member].

Programs of this nature must stake out the parameters of their activity with great care. The success of the IGRCC program is that it addresses issues of intergroup relations, conflict, and community as part of the regular curricular and student life business of the university. Although it would be reasonable for any institution to call on the expertise that is part of such a program in times of crisis over student-student or student-administration conflict, such participation would have significant impact on the subsequent credibility of the program. Under certain circumstances, the program would be looked on as an instrument of administrative control and needs rather than a program based on inquiry and open exploration of ideas and practice. In other cases, the program could appear to others to be the organizing and instigating center for student activity and protest. If brokered very carefully, individuals associated with the program might consult with interested parties as individuals, separate from their programmatic affiliation. However, programmatic involvement must be kept at a distance. The pressures can be enormous for programs to get involved in campus crises, but any apparent short-term gains are likely to result in long-term losses to the integrity and longevity of the program.

Conclusion

If West's argument (1994a) is even partially correct, that the diversity debate at its core is a struggle for the survival of American democracy, then this program and others like it are of central importance to the nation's future. That these programs should occupy a secure place in the liberal arts studies of the nation's colleges and universities makes similar good sense. Many students arriving on college campuses are intellectually ignorant and personally inexperienced in matters of intergroup relations, conflict management, and community-building. Without academic courses and safe, structured opportunities for intergroup dialogue, they will leave college unprepared to sustain a society that demands recognition of its diverse citizenry and full participation for all in its democratic structures. Experience has shown that when these learning opportunities are not available, students simply replicate in college and adult life the segregated and isolated experience of their childhood.

The work of helping students cross boundaries requires painstaking intellectual and personal effort for the professional and student staff. The IGRCC program carries a heavy time investment

158   DEMOCRATIC EDUCATION IN AN AGE OF DIFFERENCE

and emotional burden that are difficult to quantify and are also difficult to justify to those not immediately involved. The rewards are considerable, however, as one witnesses the intellectual growth and personal awakening of students from groups historically separated from one another learning to bridge differences, work through conflicts, identify commonalities, and build coalitions and friendships.

Chapter Seven

Liberal Education as Intercultural Praxis

Citizenship in a Diverse Democracy

Richard Guarasci, Grant H. Cornwell

The chapters in this book point toward a transformation in liberal education. The voices of the authors combine tones of resistance and hope, transgression and coalition. The programs are implicitly critical of the structure, curriculum, and pedagogy of the traditional university, but they do not rest content with criticism. Instead, each program is an expression of collective, creative energy, demonstrating viable, alternative models of liberal teaching and learning.

American higher education is facing many challenges as we move into the twenty-first century. Historically, it erred by positing the privileged, white, heterosexual man as the universal subject and student of science, philosophy, history, literature, and social science. Insofar as liberal education was designed to prepare students to assume citizenship in the United States, it perpetuated a monocultural and androcentric model of democracy and an ethnocentric form of patriotism. Both the educational system and the political process shared a discourse of atomistic individualism and individual competition and achievement.

Over the past thirty years, the assumed homogeneity of the educational subject and polity has broken down. If the project of liberal learning is to prepare students to live, work, and politically participate in a culturally diverse democracy, then the curriculum reforms that have occupied so much of the national press are necessary, but far from sufficient. What is taught, who is read, what questions are asked, what issues are explored—all call for continuing scrutiny. But reforming the curriculum to make it more inclusive while leaving the pedagogy—and the very structure of the university—unexamined will not further democratic aims. The experiences of students will be confused at best, counterproductive at worst. Even if some faculty do not notice the irony of studying inclusiveness, egalitarianism, and democratic participation in a classroom where the teaching is hierarchical and learning is passive, students will. To exemplify how institutions need to change if they are to educate for democracy, this book has examined programs representative of campus initiatives across the country in which curriculum and pedagogy have undergone simultaneous transformation, in which what is taught and learned has been rethought to serve more intentionally the civic mission of higher education in an intercultural democracy.

Nonetheless, these programs carry with them a certain irony. At most universities and colleges, innovative, egalitarian, and collaborative programs exist within institutions whose organizational structure speaks against the values the programs seek to promote. No matter how progressive the curriculum or empowering the pedagogy, at most colleges institutional decision making is hierarchical, resource allocation is competitive, and differences are conceptualized and treated as sources of conflict. Conflicts are often suppressed, and when they are confronted they are resolved by authority vested in bureaucratic offices. In short, very little of the functioning of university governance reflects democratic values or models democratic practices.

Faculty often experience these tensions as frustrations, and they adopt postures of resistance. In traditional colleges the domain of faculty control is the classroom; here faculty express their values through the choices they make in what and how to teach. Outside the classroom they often feel disempowered, cut off from the practices of university governance. Some faculty retreat from participation and relegate governance to those faculty and administrators they deem invested in power politics. They tend to view with cynicism or suspicion the administrative work of the university, which determines the structures within which teaching and learning take place, thus defining the boundaries of what is possible. Those who participate in governance frequently are viewed as doing so out of self-interest and personal ambition. Faculty often see committee work—the standard organizational model for university governance—as an onerous distraction and a waste of time. Participation in the community falls behind teaching and scholarship in tenure and promotion decisions. In short, faculty are often alienated from the processes that construct the conditions of their work, the conditions within which the mission of the university is pursued.

Whereas faculty distance themselves from political participation in the life of the college, students often experience institutional governance and bureaucracy as "real world" lessons on how things get done. First with confusion, later with cynical adroitness, students learn to navigate the sea of forms and offices and committees. They learn that achieving one's goals through hierarchical bureaucracies is more a function of persistence than of substance. They learn to seek out the "decision makers" rather than work in good faith with established procedures and policies. In short, they learn civic lessons that are antidemocratic. This is the sinister twist on the cliché that the most important lessons are learned outside of class; the experience many students have with university bureaucracy contributes to their cynicism about participatory citizenship.

If institutions of higher education are to prepare students to participate in democratic processes that simultaneously affirm their multiple identities and provide a common ground, those institutions are going to have to revise their hierarchical and compartmentalized ways of knowing and being. The programs described in this book offer directions for such change; the teaching and learning that goes on in them bridges many of the boundaries that mark the landscape of the contemporary university. Some of those boundaries, like that between academic and student affairs divisions, are fairly recent historical developments; others, like that between faculty and students, or books and experience, date back to the medieval origins of the university.

By building bridges and making connections, the programs call into question established hierarchies and domains of authority, and the challenges they present to traditional educational structures do provoke criticism. On their home campuses, faculty often mark their educational politics by taking a stance for or against these programs; the programs have supporters who see them as the vanguard of progressive reforms, and detractors who view them as undermining certain core values of university teaching and scholarship. But if we map the bridges and survey the new educational landscape posited by these programs, we glimpse universities as they would look if their missions were seriously understood to be preparing students for participating in an intercultural democracy.

All of the programs seek to bridge one of the most rigid structural boundaries in the contemporary college or university, the boundary between academic and student affairs. This division is the final triumph of the mind-body dualism posited by Descartes; faculty are to be concerned with the life of the mind, student development professionals with the behavior of bodies and emotions. This bifurcation and the concomitant professionalization of faculty and staff has led to sharply conflicting models for treatment of students. The division of labor suggests that students are budding intellects to their professors, and bodies requiring dormitory rooms, counseling, discipline, nurturance, and entertainment to the student affairs administrators. Professors tend to approach their interactions with students with one set of practices, student affairs personnel with another, and these practices are sometimes in conflict with each other. In the academic arena students are judged and held accountable with objectivity operating as the normative ideal; work is to be evaluated on its merits, abstracted from the students who produced it, their backgrounds, their emotional lives. On the other hand, within student affairs, especially in counseling, students' subjectivity is the primary focus of concern.

When faculty and student affairs people come together in joint projects, both methodologies are called into question, as neither alone is adequate to the process of educating a human being. The programs described in this book are, in this sense, post-Cartesian; they take a more holistic approach toward students and toward education itself. They entail critical examination of how lived experience embodies abstract ideas. A recent visitor to St. Lawrence remarked that the First-Year Program appears to have taken away most of the creative work usually done by student affairs professionals. This perception betrays how deeply the divisions of labor are ingrained in our understanding of university work. This visitor was unable to see that everything that happens in the program is the result of collaboration between the persons who work in it, some of whom are trained in student development, some in academic disciplines. At its best, that collaboration has produced a new set of practices for educating students, one that does not break up into easily recognized "student affairs" and "faculty" roles.

The Program on Intergroup Relations, Conflict, and Community at the University of Michigan also depends on this post-Cartesian collaboration between academic affairs and student affairs, grounding its intergroup dialogues in the intellectual framework of courses on diversity, and practicing what is learned in the classroom about cultural differences in face-to-face conversations that explore emotions and values. Group process and critical reflection on theory and literature mutually inform one another, thus bridging the work of the counselor and the teacher. As in St. Lawrence's program, at Michigan experienced students serve as peer leaders, altering many of the hierarchies that structure the educational system.

If we begin with the assumption that Descartes got it wrong, that the mind-body dualism is obsolete as a view of the person, then dividing the work of the university between academic and student affairs is not the way to go. It is a cliché to say that we should treat students as whole persons, yet the kinds of programs discussed in this book stand out because they actually do it; they refuse to partition students into classroom intellects and campus bodies. Ideas are not relegated to the classroom; experience is not left devalued and unexamined.

These programs do more than reach across the faculty–student affairs boundary; by invoking student experience and working with it critically, they transgress the domain of texts as the loci of knowledge. Reading remains central to the teaching and learning process, but in these programs what is read is placed in dialectic tension with student experience. In the service learning programs at both Rutgers and Hobart and William Smith, students come to understand the contexts of the community service work through rigorous course work in social and political theory. Service learning is a reconceptualization of an old idea, that of students volunteering in local communities. It is new enough that it does not yet have a predictable place on the university landscape. At some institutions it is administered under the student affairs division, at others under academic affairs. But the label, and the construct it represents, is precisely one that brings together academic and student affairs, classroom learning and experience, the curricular and the extracurricular. Whereas traditional community service took place outside the domain of faculty—in Greek houses, chaplain's offices, or student organizations—it has now became matter for critical and theoretical reflection in courses. Service work can be a "lab" for a course, or a course can be an adjunct to a service project. But service learning fits comfortably in neither domain; its work bridges the division, but it is clearly now educational in its mission. As the chapter on the women's studies program at Rutgers emphasizes, the community being "served" is now considered a teaching partner, not a needy recipient of charity. There is a world of difference between reinforcing inequality by sending privileged students out to "help the needy" and engaging students in an experiential learning project that produces better understanding and respect on both sides, the kind of intercultural mutuality that must ground democratic practice.

The Rutgers women's studies internship is one part of a university-wide Citizenship and Service Education (CASE) program, so students read and write about citizenship and democracy. The emphasis on feminism and women's issues challenges traditional theories of democracy. But in both the Hobart and William Smith program and that at Rutgers, students are encouraged to judge the adequacy of democratic theory by measuring it against their personal experiences in the community. Similarly, in the living-learning program at St. Lawrence, some students study the history of social contract theory in a course while drafting and implementing their own social contract for how they will live together. Again, ideas read are transformed when they become ideas lived.

These programs promote critical reflection on interpersonal experiences of difference. They use the classroom to connect theoretical readings with the autobiographical narratives of students, to make sure students are processing their community encounters in a constructive and critical way, and to help students refrain from stereotyping those they meet in the community. Encountering differences, both within oneself and in others, can be a challenging and disruptive experience. Lacking a critical framework, such experiences have the potential to reinforce prejudices and close people off from new experiences. The autobiographical narratives cited in this book demonstrate the potential these experiential courses have for transforming students and building mutual relationships among people who would otherwise be kept separate by boundaries of many kinds. Certainly one hope of service learning projects is that students' capacities for empathy will become more general and will reach beyond the particular relationships of the students' service work. If universities are to play a role in envisioning an intercultural democratic society, one in which citizens treat each other with respect and identify with one another across differences, they cannot wall themselves off from the communities surrounding them or have exclusive class divisions between all of the persons who work within them. Service learning programs suggest ways in which these boundaries can become more permeable.

In fact, all of the programs examined here seek to transform the relationship of persons to one another. The programs share an epistemology that is communal and collaborative, owing much to the work of feminist pedagogies. In the academy there is a certain persistence of the view that knowledge is the product of individual genius; indeed, it remains the case that most faculty labor alone as scholars, often in competition with their peers. The programs described in this book suggest that some knowledge cannot be gained except through collaboration. It is the underlying premise of the work with intergroup relations at the University of Michigan that there is no blueprint for how persons who differ from one another in multiple dimensions can form democratic communities. That knowledge has to be worked out through the collaboration of those committed to it. The collaborative pedagogies practiced at LaGuardia Community College not only have kept students engaged in their learning when they might have otherwise dropped out, but also have shown that students can make more progress working in collaboration than they can alone in competition with one another.

Finally, we think it is important to notice the multiple creative and productive ways in which the programs bridge the boundaries between disciplines. The women's studies program at Rutgers has pioneered in the creation of interdisciplinary knowledge. When feminist scholars began the task of recovering the erased histories of and texts by women, they soon found that traditional historical and disciplinary boundaries did not fit the material with which they were working, that the disciplines themselves were constructed along heavy gender lines. Emerging scholarship about other underrepresented groups and cultures continues to undermine the sanctity of traditional disciplinary epistemologies.

The "writing across the curriculum" movement is another bridge that crosses disciplinary divides. Through it, the traditional segmentation of students' intellectual work into skill development—with writing instruction taking place in one department, oral communication instruction in another—and substantive inquiry elsewhere altogether, is being undone in various programs across the country. All of the work represented in this book has been influenced by and contributes to this movement, though perhaps LaGuardia Community College and St. Lawrence University have built the most self-conscious links between the teaching of content and skills.

Although each program has emerged out of local and particular circumstances, each also exemplifies and interconnects with national movements to reform education in general and to use education to revitalize democracy in particular. These programs answer bell hooks's call in *Teaching to Transgress*: "Urging all of us to open our minds and hearts so that we can know beyond the boundaries of what is acceptable, so that we can think and rethink, so that we can create new visions, I celebrate teaching that enables transgressions—a movement against and beyond boundaries. It is that movement which makes education the practice of freedom" (1994, p. 12).

A number of foundations have created initiatives to encourage and support these kinds of efforts. These include the National Endowment for the Humanities (NEH) American Conversation Project, the Ford Foundation's Diversity Project, the Association of American Colleges and Universities (AAC&U) American Commitments Project, the American Association of Higher Education's (AAHE) service learning project, and the Association of Historically Black College's (HBC) service learning project. Innovative and radical programs depend on these foundations, not just for money but for a dialogical relationship and a sense of community. Small groups of faculty and staff creating initiatives at a college need to be connected to wider networks of colleagues engaged in similar work. As part of a national project, they participate in workshops and conferences that give them feedback on what they are doing, offer theoretical and political insights on curricular and pedagogical reform, and most important, create a larger community of colleagues sharing similar goals.

To take one example, the AAC&U American Commitments Project has spurred almost two hundred colleges to think about the meaning, goals, and needs of U.S. democracy in a time of

fragmentation and identity politics. It has offered several long, substantive faculty development seminars, providing a collection of
important readings on democracy and difference. It has developed
a series of papers on issues of curriculum development for citizenship in a diverse democracy, modeling participatory democracy in
the writing process. The papers were drafted collaboratively, then
circulated at conferences for discussion and critique over a period
of several years. Their final form is the product of extensive rewriting that shows the input of many, many members of AAC&U.

The colleges and universities in the project have been supported in the development of their individual programs by the
workshops and conferences and by peer evaluation. This is a model
of democracy that also appreciates and fosters differences. In no
way does AAC&U develop a master blueprint for every program.
Each school works within its own identity, location, demographics,
resources, and ethos. What is suitable for an urban community college in Southern California is not going to work at a private liberal
arts college in Massachusetts or at a big state university in Michigan. Yet each of these colleges participating in American Commitments is working with a shared goal: that of educating students
to be active and responsible and equal participants in U.S. citizenship, participants who embrace all kinds of differences while standing on common ground.

Because in many regards we are not all equal, especially in our
status and resources as institutions of higher learning, having community college faculty discuss common goals with elite college faculty is a key step in envisioning how to educate students for
democracy. Faculty themselves are not free of elitism, racism, or
sexism. National conferences that demand of faculty and of administrators intercultural dialogue and shared analysis of diverse types
of educational missions serve to educate the faculty in the same
way that faculty need to educate students.

Representative of some of the best new initiatives fostered by
national foundations, the programs described in this book offer partial visions of a democratic college, one organized without rigid

divisions, departments, and hierarchies of authority. Such a college would enable students and faculty to experience their work as genuine participation in a democratic community. Commitments to inclusivity and collaboration would permeate the institutional ethos. Governance and decision making would be seen not as peripheral tasks necessary to the real work of the university but as part of that real work. Democratic decision making and all genuinely collaborative work are notorious for the time they demand. When the work to be done is seen as unimportant or necessary but uninteresting, inclusive, collaborative processes seem grossly inefficient. However, if every instance when students, faculty, and staff sit down to work on something together is seen as an occasion to practice the skills and embody the values the university exists to promote, then the analysis of efficiency has to be recast. Committee meetings—not only those on curriculum, hiring, and tenure but also those on budget, campus issues, and physical plant—all have the potential to be venues for teaching and learning, for engaging in a kind of experiential inquiry into ideas and values.

Each of the bridges built by these exemplary programs is reconstructive: boundaries are crossed so that artificial separations can be rejoined, perhaps even healed. Bodies and minds can learn together; students and faculty can learn and teach together; campus and community can learn from each other. Mutual respect and understanding can supplant exclusion, individual competition, and exploitation. In the university transformed, everyone would be seen as a teacher, everyone a learner. The faculty's purview over the curriculum and the student development staff's purview over the co-curriculum would dissolve into shared responsibility for campus life, inside the classroom and out. This kind of negotiated, comprehensive institution would still recognize that we come to our work with different kinds of professional training. The intellectual demands and training of faculty contribute much-needed critical scrutiny to received notions that help perpetuate the inequalities and alienations of the society in which we live. Faculty contribute skills and knowledge needed to create new worlds.

But student affairs professionals can remind faculty and students that we are all people with emotional lives and bodies that need nourishing, that academic learning must take into account the real needs of real people and help them live their lives. Similarly, experiential learning brings theories down to earth, to practices and persons. But critical scrutiny prevents experience from perpetuating stereotypes or from being overgeneralized. It examines the lenses through which the perceiver observes experience. And again, as the programs described in this book have shown, the knowledge and practices that evolve out of crossing boundaries far exceed the sums of the programs' parts. In drawing on this diversity of perspectives and in bringing together the differences into collaborative educational work, the kinds of alternative universities these programs suggest would model the democratic processes we seek as a nation.

References

Aisenberg, N., and Harrington, M. *Women of Academe: Outsiders in the Sacred Grove*. Amherst: University of Massachusetts Press, 1988.

American Commitments National Panel. *American Pluralism, American Commitments and the College Curriculum*. Draft report. Washington, D.C.: Association of American Colleges, 1995a.

American Commitments National Panel. *Diversity, Democracy, and Higher Education: A Meeting Ground for American Pluralism*. Draft report. Washington, D.C.: Association of American Colleges, 1995b.

Anzaldua, G. *Borderlands/La Frontera: The New Mestiza*. San Francisco: Aunt Lute Books, 1987.

Astin, A. *What Matters in College: Four Critical Years Revisited*. San Francisco: Jossey-Bass, 1993.

Atlas, J. *The Book Wars*. New York: Whittle Direct Books, 1990.

Bann, S. *Russian Formalism: A Collection of Articles and Texts in Translation*. Lanham, Md.: Barnes & Noble Books, 1973.

Barber, B. R. "Neither Leaders nor Followers: Citizenship Under Strong Democracy." In B. R. Barber and R. M. Battistoni (eds.), *Education for Democracy*. Dubuque, Iowa: Kendall/Hunt, 1993, pp. 161–170.

Barber, B. R., and Battistoni, R. M. "A Season of Service: Introducing Service Learning into the Liberal Arts Curriculum." *PS: Political Science and Politics*, June 1993, pp. 235–240.

Bellah, R. N., and others. *Habits of the Heart*. Berkeley: University of California Press, 1985.

Bennett, W. *The Book of Virtues*. New York: Simon & Schuster, 1993.

Bloom, A. *The Closing of the American Mind*. New York: Simon & Schuster, 1987.

Boyer, E. *College: The Undergraduate Experience in America*. New York: HarperCollins, 1987.

Boyte, H. "Practical Politics." Cited in B. R. Barber and R. M. Battistoni, "A Season of Service: Introducing Service Learning into the Liberal Arts Curriculum." *PS: Political Science and Politics*, June 1993, pp. 235–240.

Brownmiller, S. *Femininity*. New York: Simon & Schuster, 1984.

Bruffee, K. "Collaborative Learning and the Conversation of Mankind." *College English*, 1984, 46(7), 640–648.

Bruffee, K. *Collaborative Learning: Higher Education, Interdependence and the Authority of Knowledge*. Baltimore, Md.: Johns Hopkins University Press, 1993.

Buckley, W. F. *Gratitude*. New York: Random House, 1990.

Campus Compact. *Service Counts: Lessons from the Field of Service and Higher Education*. Providence, R.I.: Campus Compact, 1995.

Coles, R. *The Call of Service*. Boston: Houghton Mifflin, 1993.

Collins, P. H. "Learning from the Outsider Within: The Sociological Significance of Black Feminist Thought." *Social Problems*, Oct.-Dec. 1986, pp. 14–32.

Commission on National and Community Service. "What You Can Do for Your Country." *Annual Report*. Washington, D.C.: Commission on National and Community Service, Jan. 1993.

Culley, M., and Portuges, C. *Gendered Subjects: The Dynamics of Feminist Teaching*. New York: Routledge, 1985.

Damrosch, D. "The Scholar as Exile: Learning to Love Loneliness." *Lingua Franca*, 1995, 5(2), 56–60.

Derrida, J. *Of Grammatology* (G. Spivak, trans.). Baltimore, Md.: Johns Hopkins University Press, 1976.

Derrida, J. *Writing and Difference* (A. Bass, trans.). Chicago: University of Chicago Press, 1978.

Dewey, J. *Human Nature and Conduct*. New York: Random House, 1957.

Dewey, J. *Democracy and Education*. New York: Free Press, 1966. (Originally published 1916.)

D'Souza, D. *Illiberal Education: The Politics of Race and Sex on Campus*. New York: Free Press, 1991.

DuBois, E., and others. *Feminist Scholarship: Kindling in the Groves of Academe*. Urbana and Chicago: University of Illinois Press, 1987.

Etzioni, A. *The Spirit of Community: Rights, Responsibilities and the Communitarian Agenda*. New York: Crown, 1993.

Fanon, F. *The Wretched of the Earth* (C. Farington, trans.). New York: Grove Press, 1968. (Originally published 1963.)

Flax, J. "Women Do Theory." In A. M. Jaggar and P. S. Rothenberg (eds.), *Feminist Frameworks: Alternative Theoretical Accounts of the Relations Between Women and Men*. 3rd Ed. New York: McGraw Hill, 1993, 80–85.

Foucault, M. *Language, Counter-Memory, Practice: Selected Essays and Interviews* (D. Bouchard and S. Simon, trans.).Ithaca, N.Y.: Cornell University Press, 1977.

Foucault, M. *Power/Knowledge: Selected Interviews and Other Writings, 1972–1977* (C. Gordon, trans.). New York: Pantheon, 1980.

Frankel, N., and Dye, N. S. (eds.). *Gender, Class, Race, and Reform in the Progressive Era.* Lexington: University Press of Kentucky, 1991.

Gabriel, S. L., and Smithson, I. *Gender in the Classroom: Power and Pedagogy.* Urbana: University of Illinois Press, 1991.

Gamson, Z. "Collaborative Learning Comes of Age." *Change: The Magazine of Higher Learning,* 1994, *26*(5), 44–49.

Gates, H. L., Jr. *Loose Canons: Notes on the Culture Wars.* New York: Oxford University Press, 1992.

Gilligan, C. *In a Different Voice: Psychological Theory and Women's Development.* Cambridge, Mass.: Harvard University Press, 1982.

Ginzberg, L. D. *Women and the Work of Benevolence: Morality, Politics, and Class in the Nineteenth-Century United States.* New Haven, Conn.: Yale University Press, 1991.

Giroux, H. A. "Resisting Difference: Cultural Studies and the Discourse of Critical Pedagogy." In L. Grossberg, C. Nelson, and P. Treichler (eds.), *Cultural Studies.* New York: Routledge, 1992.

Goldberg, V. "The Soup-Kitchen Classroom." *New York Times Magazine,* Sept. 27, 1992, p. 50.

Griffin, G. B. *Calling: Essays on Teaching in the Mother Tongue.* Pasadena, Calif.: Trilogy Books, 1993.

Guarasci, R., and Cornwell, G. H. "Democratic Education in an Age of Difference." *Perspectives,* 1993, *23*(1), 6–13.

Guarasci, R., and Rimmerman, C. "Democratic Learning in a Microcosm of Post Industrial America." In T. Becker (ed.), *Teaching Democracy by Being Democratic.* New York: Praeger, 1997.

Gurin, P., Nagda, B., Lopez, G., and Sfeir-Younis, L. "Diversity and Multicultural Curriculum: Understanding Social Causation." *Michigan Journal of Political Science,* Spring 1993, no. 16.

Hacker, A. *Two Nations: Black and White, Separate, Hostile, Unequal.* New York: Scribner, 1992.

Harding, S. *Whose Science? Whose Knowledge? Thinking from Women's Lives.* Ithaca, N.Y.: Cornell University Press, 1991.

Hochschild, A. *The Second Shift.* New York: Avon, 1989.

hooks, b. *Teaching to Transgress: Education as the Practice of Freedom.* New York: Routledge, 1994.

Horwitz, M. "New Student Seminar in New Student House: Violence." *Notes From the Field: Reflections of Collaborative Learning at LaGuardia.* LaGuardia College internal publication, Spring 1994, pp. 66–69.

Hutchins, R. M. *The Higher Learning in America.* New Haven, Conn.: Yale University Press, 1936.

Kessler-Harris, A. "The View from Women's Studies." *Signs*, Summer 1992, pp. 794–805.

Light, R. *Explorations with Students and Faculty About Teaching, Learning and Student Life.* The Harvard Assessment Seminars, no. 1. Cambridge, Mass.: Graduate School of Education, Harvard University, 1990.

Light, R. *Explorations with Students and Faculty About Teaching, Learning and Student Life.* The Harvard Assessment Seminars, no. 2. Cambridge, Mass.: Graduate School of Education, Harvard University, 1991.

Lorde, A. *Sister Outsider.* Freedom, Calif.: Crossing Press, 1984.

Lorde, A. "Age, Race, Class, and Sex: Women Redefining Difference." In B. Balliet and D. Humphreys (eds.), *Women, Culture and Society: A Reader.* Dubuque, Iowa: Kendall/Hunt, 1992.

Maher, F. A., and Tetreault, M.K.T. *The Feminist Classroom.* New York: Basic Books, 1994.

Massey, D., and Denton, N. *American Apartheid.* Cambridge, Mass.: Harvard University Press, 1993.

Matthews, R. S., and Associates. *Case Studies: Teaching at LaGuardia Community College.* New York: LaGuardia Community College, Summer 1994a.

Matthews, R. S., and Associates. *Notes from the Field: Reflections on Collaborative Learning at LaGuardia.* New York: LaGuardia Community College, Spring 1994b.

Meiklejohn, A. *The Experimental College.* New York: HarperCollins, 1932.

Miller, G. E. *The Meaning of General Education.* New York: Teachers College Press, 1988.

Milstein, S. "Foundations: A History of the First Ten Years of Women's Studies at Rutgers University." Senior honors thesis, Rutgers University, 1993.

Minnich, E., O'Barr, J., and Rosenfeld, R. (eds.). *Reconstructing the Academy: Women's Education and Women's Studies.* Chicago: University of Chicago Press, 1988.

Moffat, M. *Coming of Age in New Jersey: College and American Culture.* New Brunswick, N.J.: Rutgers University Press, 1989.

Monaco, N. M., and Gaier, E. L. "Single-Sex Versus Coeducational Environment and Achievement in Adolescent Females." *Adolescence*, Fall 1992, 27, 579–594.

Nagda, B., Zuniga, X., and Sevig, T. "Bridging Differences Through Peer Facilitated Intergroup Dialogues." In S. Hatcher (ed.), *Peer Programs on a College Campus: Theory, Training and the Voices of the Peers.* San Diego, Calif.: New Resources, 1995.

Ngugi wa Thiong'o. "On the Abolition of the English Department." *Homecoming Essays.* London: Heinemann, 1972.

Noddings, N. *Caring: A Feminine Approach to Ethics.* Berkeley: University of California Press, 1984.

Orenstein, G. "The Master Plan for Women's Studies." Unpublished document, Women's Studies Program, Rutgers University, 1976–77.

Pagano, J. A. *Exiles and Communities: Teaching in the Patriarchal Wilderness.* Albany: SUNY Press, 1990.

Program on Intergroup Relations and Conflict. *What Is an Intergroup Dialogue?* Flier. Ann Arbor: University of Michigan, 1993.

Sandler, B., and others. *The Classroom Climate: A Chilly One for Women?* Washington, D. C.: Association of American Colleges Project on the Status and Education of Women, 1984.

Saussure, D., de. *Course in General Linguistics* (W. Baskin, trans.). New York: Philosophical Library, 1959.

Schlesinger, A. *The Disuniting of America.* New York: Norton, 1991.

Schoem, D. (ed.). *Inside Separate Worlds: Life Stories of Young Blacks, Jews, and Latinos.* Ann Arbor: University of Michigan Press, 1991.

Schoem, D., Frankel, L., Zuniga, X., and Lewis, E. (eds.). *Multicultural Teaching in the University.* New York: Praeger, 1993.

Schuster, M. R., and Van Dyne, S. R. *Women's Place in the Academy: Transforming the Liberal Arts Curriculum.* Lanham, Md.: Rowman & Littlefield, 1985.

Sidel, R. *Battling Bias: The Struggle for Identity and Community on College Campuses.* New York: Viking Penguin, 1994.

Spitzberg, I. J., Jr., and Thorndike, V. V. *Creating Community on College Campuses.* Albany: SUNY Press, 1992.

Spivak, G. C. *In Other Worlds: Essays in Cultural Politics.* London: Methuen, 1987.

"Statement of Philosophy and Goals for the Residential Component of the FYP at St. Lawrence University." Canton, N.Y.: St. Lawrence University, 1993.

Stimpson, C. "Some Comments on the Curriculum: Can We Get Beyond Our Controversies?" *Change,* 1992a, 2(4), 9–11, 53.

Stimpson, C. "The White Squares: Helping Students Fill in the Blanks." *Change,* 1992b, 24(1), 77.

Sykes, C. *Profscam: Professors and the Demise of Higher Education.* New York: St. Martin's Press, 1988.

Taylor, C. *Multiculturalism and the Politics of Recognition.* Princeton, N.J.: Princeton University Press, 1992.

Terkel, S. *American Dreams: Lost and Found.* New York: Pantheon Books, 1980.

Terkel, S. *Race: How Blacks and Whites Think and Feel About the American Obsession.* New York: New Press, 1992.

Tierney, W. G. *Curricular Landscapes, Democratic Vistas: Transformative Leadership in Higher Education.* New York: Praeger, 1989.

Tinto, V. *Leaving College: Rethinking the Causes and Cures of Student Attrition.* Chicago: University of Chicago Press, 1987.

Tinto, V., Goodsell, A., and Russo, P. *Building Learning Communities for New College Students: A Summary of Research Findings of the Collaborative Learning Project.* Syracuse, N.Y.: National Center on Postsecondary Teaching, Learning and Assessment, Syracuse University, 1994.

Trimbur, J. "Consensus and Difference in Collaborative Learning." *College English*, 1989, *51*(6), 602–616.

West, C. *Prophetic Thought in Postmodern Times*. Monroe, Maine: Common Courage Press, 1993a.

West, C. *Race Matters*. Boston: Beacon Press, 1993b.

West, C. "Race and Social Justice in America." *Liberal Education*, 1994a, 80(3), 32–39.

West, C. *Race Matters*. New York: Vintage Press, 1994b.

Zuniga, X., and Nagda, B. A. "Dialogue Groups: An Innovative Approach to Multicultural Learning." In D. Schoem, L. Frankel, X. Zuniga, and E. Lewis, *Multicultural Teaching in the University*. New York: Praeger, 1993.

Index